Retirement Hell

Byproduct of a Middle Class under Siege

Don Pollock CPA

Retirement Hell - Byproduct of a Middle Class under Siege

Copyrighted © 2017 by Don Pollock

Publisher CTP Press

London

Requests can be directed to the publisher CTP Press at ctppublisher@gmail.com

Don can be contacted at don.retirementhell@gmail.com

First Edition

ISBN   978-0-9959105-1-5

Website   donpollock.com

Cover Design by Kelly Hunt

To my parents, Maxine and Cecil Pollock
and my friend Bailey who left this world too early

Feedback

The author encourages feedback from our readers, especially potential solutions to issues that were raised in this book. You can contact the author directly, or there is a discussion forum on our website where readers can share their views.

Website   donpollock.com

Password   family

CONTENTS

What is Retirement Hell?

It is that phase of life when retired individuals lack the money to maintain a dignified lifestyle and must rely on government assistance to pay their bills. It will include many hard-working families that were able to maintain a satisfactory lifestyle during their working years, but due to a lack of savings and pension income, they are unable to fund a retirement that may last over thirty years. If government pensions are your primary source of income, it will be a challenge to enjoy retirement while living in poverty.

If you only had three takeaways from this book, please believe the following statements are true:

1. Unless you are wealthy, a high-income earner or a member of a generous defined benefit pension plan, it will be a struggle to fund the retirement of your dreams. The situation may be worse for our children and grandchildren.

2. The middle class is under siege and this will be a key factor in the inability of many families to fund their retirement. It will also change the political landscape as the underclass is attaining a critical mass.

3. The baby boomer's formula for financial success is obsolete and it has been replaced by a new formula that will be challenging to implement.

INTRODUCTION

The accuracy of forecasting has been compared to monkeys throwing darts at a wall and given the hidden agenda of many forecasters; monkeys may have a better track record. Although I understand the problems related to accurate predictions, if certain trends are extrapolated forward for a few decades, we shall face a major crisis. A demographic spike known as the baby boomers is retiring and the mess they leave behind will handcuff attempts by future generations to define their destiny. I shall share a vision of the future that is not optimistic for a growing segment of the population and I fear my generation lacks the expertise to resolve these issues.

My background has its roots in a working-class family from the beautiful town of Goderich, Ontario. I was able to translate an absolute lack of exceptionalism in high school into a career that included graduating from an elite business school, obtaining my CPA/CA degree and working for a world class company in the areas of taxation and pensions. I also owned a publishing company that provided tax and financial information to many of the country's largest businesses and successful entrepreneurs for over three decades. Only much later in life did I realize that any successes achieved were primarily the result of being a member of the luckiest generation in history. We were provided with opportunities that with minimal effort could be transformed into some level of financial success. During this journey, I was fortunate to encounter many gifted individuals and their wisdom, experience and insights are woven throughout these pages and I am thankful for their input.

Economists subdivide families into various groups such as middle class, working families, working poor, professionals, the underemployed, the top 1%, etc. Such classifications are normally based on income levels or type of employment. A typical definition of middle class would be incomes that fall in the range of twice the median income at the top end and two-thirds of the median as the lowest qualifying income. Thus, if the median income were $50,000, the middle class would be defined as those earning between $33,333 and $100,000. We are not defining middle class as a group that fits within a certain income range; rather it refers to families that meet the following criteria:

- They earn sufficient income to support their family without government assistance. We are ignoring the wealthy in this analysis.
- They share middle-class values. This includes a work ethic, a belief that the harder they work, the more likely they are to be successful and goals can be achieved by following the rules.

As for our future economy, it is a classic good news, bad news story. The good news is that it will include a strong and vibrant middle class; unfortunately, many families will struggle to maintain their former standard of living. As the number of people retiring continues to increase at a time when many families are sliding down the economic ladder, the taxes of a financially stressed middle class must support an ever-expanding group that requires government assistance. Consumer spending is a major driver of the economy and any slowdown will have a negative impact on businesses and government revenue.

Families that have accumulated a reasonable level of financial security should be concerned about a struggling middle class. Even if their future unfolds as planned, they can still be impacted as those who are struggling may not accept their fate. Whether they take to the streets or organize politically, they have sufficient mass to upset the status quo. Their choices for political leaders may have an autocratic nature and policies may favor a redistribution of income from the haves to the have-nots. It is naïve to believe your family is sufficiently insulated, or your children's future is secure if all hell breaks out. Uprisings, protests and repressed anger by a large number of people who are devoid of hope and opportunity will not be resolved without some innocent victims.

The surge in manufacturing that resulted from the increased demand following the Second World War was a key reason for the formation of our middle class. Jobs were plentiful and neither an education nor a high level of skill was necessary to support a family. When low-skilled manufacturing jobs started to disappear and the replacement jobs did not provide the same level of compensation, middle-class families were often overextended and a secure lifestyle could no longer be guaranteed. For many families, funding a retirement that may last over thirty years will often require government assistance. It is all but impossible to have the retirement of your dreams, or even a dignified retirement if the only source of income is a government pension. This book will explore these issues and outline a formula to achieve success in our fast-paced future.

Worldview is a term that encompasses our attitudes, beliefs and interpretation of reality. We determine what we believe to be true by processing information from various sources. However, if we live in a post-truth society where many of the messages received are not statements of absolute truth, but rather are puffery, opinions and biased information, who and what can we believe? When listening to the words of politicians, advertisements, corporations and the media, we understand their words cannot always be taken at face value. I will share a worldview that can be summarized by an old hockey adage - keep your head up when you cross the blue line.

PART ONE

HOW WE ARRIVED AT THIS POINT

This section outlines how boomers became the most privileged generation in history. However, the good times came to an end for many working families and they face an uncertain future. This section reviews how these circumstances came to exist.

CHAPTER ONE

LUNCH

All things being equal, the person with the best mom wins

Three groups of friends are meeting at separate locations for lunch and despite differences in age and lifestyle, their parents are from working-class families. Two groups are members of the boomer's generation, while the other consists of young men in their early thirties. One man from each group comes from the same neighborhood in a small town, but decisions they made as teenagers started them on very different journeys through life.

Lunch at the Club - After a round of golf at a private club, four friends enjoy a beer and discuss upcoming plans. They travel a few times per year, usually to Europe or some exotic locale. They drive imported vehicles and live in fine neighborhoods. Their children have completed university, but few have launched successful careers. They have investment portfolios, generous pensions and not a financial care in the world. Although they face the normal stresses of everyday life, their financial future is secure and their children should receive significant inheritances. Even though money is not a concern for this group, there are threads of the conversation that tie back to their working-class roots. One individual collects coupons on future rounds of golf, while another buys demo golf clubs. They consider themselves thrifty and will continue to save a buck here and another buck there while planning a trip to Europe. Their parents were thrifty and they take pride in saving money, even if it is not necessary. Although some wealthy people are extravagant and highly leveraged, it's amazing how many financial secure people are frugal. Billionaire Warren Buffet lives in a home in Omaha that was purchased in the 1950s and Boone Pickens brags of wearing ten-year-old suits.

This scene is being played out in various clubs, restaurants and vacation spots across North America. These boomers were successful throughout their careers and are enjoying a retirement that far exceeds that of their parents. Life is good.

Lunch at the Legion - In another world, about a million miles away across the county line, four friends are enjoying lunch at the Legion. A few beers, a quick game of darts and at 2:00 pm the euchre tournament starts. The conversation includes plans for upcoming camping trips and a possible family vacation to Florida. They speak with pride of their family and sports teams. These men lost their jobs when their plant closed in the previous decade and although they were able to find some part-time employment, who wants to hire a sixty-year-old? They have lovely homes, drive older domestic cars and are entering a retirement that will be modest. There is no resentment aimed at the owners of the plant that moved their jobs overseas or the bankers, politicians, or immigrants that are often blamed for economic restructuring. There is a sense that fate worked against them through no fault of their own.

They enjoyed well-paying manufacturing jobs and when the plant was open, no one complained about their lifestyle. As for retirement, the future is uncertain and a little bit scary. They are fortunate that they were downsized in the latter part of their careers. Their greatest fear is that they will live for another thirty years and once their spouse passes away they will end up in a nursing home sharing a room with three strangers.

This group consists of middle-class survivors. Although their reasonable paying jobs were eliminated, they still consider themselves part of the middle class as they had a safety net. At the time they lost their jobs, they had accumulated some assets and paid off the mortgage. Their income was reduced, but their spouses were employed and their children have left the nest which allows them to maintain an acceptable version of their former lifestyle.

Worlds Apart, but Still Connected - Two friends grew up in a working-class neighborhood. They played sports, drank beer, chased girls and for the most part stayed out of trouble. They lived the life of many young men in the 1960s and 1970s. They were typical baby boomers, although it was a term that was not part of their vocabulary. They were working-class kids enjoying a childhood that would define a part of their character. Neither young man was a scholar, but they passed each grade. They were probably equal in terms of intelligence, character and work ethic. They graduated high school and then their worlds drifted apart. One started working at the local factory and received a reasonable salary that was sufficient to fund the lifestyle of a single man enjoying his youth. He married, had children and lived a comfortable life. Then all hell broke loose when the plant closed and although the house was paid off, future pension benefits would be meager. If the plant had not closed, the family's retirement would be more secure. Circumstances beyond his control kicked him in the gut and he has been forced into an uncertain, but satisfactory lifestyle. He made good decisions at every point in his life, but negative global forces landed on his doorstep.

The other young man left town to attend university. He was not as strong or athletic as his friend who took the factory job and this may have made manual labor less appealing. In this period, almost everyone who graduated high school could go to university as the entrance requirements were minimal. Four years later with a university degree in hand, the young man from the small town and his fellow graduates were in demand. Employers were offering large salaries and generous pension plans. At the time they were hired, very few gave pension benefits a second thought. The new job meant a cool car, great apartment and a starting salary that exceeded his father's pay even though his dad had worked for over twenty-five years. Once hired, there were opportunities for promotion and management positions. Rather than receiving an annual inflationary pay raise, the promotions and salary increases were significant. Most of the other employees did not have a university degree, so competition for promotions was not severe.

Now forty-five years after leaving high school, the former factory worker and university graduate are still friends. Their children have left home and they are both retired. How did they spend their time yesterday? One was having lunch at a private golf club discussing plans with three friends, while the other was finishing his beer at the Legion. One chap faces a retirement in which finances are a concern, whereas the other understands there are issues to be faced as we age, but it does not include a lack of money. Two friends of equal intelligence and work effort made different choices at the age of eighteen. If we measure success by who has the most toys when they die, the university graduate wins, but he is very open about why he was successful. He was lucky. He was privileged to be a member of the luckiest generation that ever lived and he backed into a wealth creation formula that he did not know existed.

Like most students of their day, these young men were focused on friends, sports and girls. Bragging of conquests that never happened, punching above their weight and not believing they landed a few blows, while not caring about the good ones that got away. They lacked a plan for the future, but that was not necessary for boomers. If they wanted to go to university, they just picked a school and usually got accepted. If they wanted a job in a factory, apply and most were hired. There was so much low-hanging fruit; it was a matter of picking an opportunity and following that path into the workforce. There were gifted students and some with less obvious academic abilities, but those in the middle that chose to pursue a higher education were able to excel. Looking back at my peers in high school, I had two friends who were at the opposite ends of the academic spectrum. I was convinced one was so brilliant that a Nobel Prize in science would be part of his future and the other could lift heavy objects. The future Nobel Prize winner never left his hometown and he made a living in a low paying menial job. As for the lifter of heavy things, he traveled the world and has insight into the issues of the day that far exceeded my perception of his skill set. Boomers did not have to be born into wealthy families or be especially gifted academically to achieve incredible success. Often all they had to do was show up and the prize was there for the taking.

One interesting point of comparison is there no difference in the paths followed by the children of these two groups having lunch. All of their children obtained a post-secondary school education. These men shared middle-class values, one of which is to assist and support their children in attaining an education. Gone are the days that if the father worked in the plant or mine, it was expected the son would follow in his footsteps. These men are all members of the middle class and they share its values.

They took different paths through life, but their values remained intact.

Lunch at the Diner - There was a third group having lunch that day at the diner down the street from the Legion. These men were from the same town, graduated from the same high school and worked in the same factory as the men having lunch at the Legion. They are just thirty years younger. Although the meeting was called lunch, it was a plate of fries and multiple rounds of beer. One young man lives with his parents, one is divorced and the other two live with lady friends. They all have fathered at least one child. One has a part-time delivery job; two survive on welfare, while the fourth is unable to work because of a bad back. Fortunately, disability insurance pays about the same as a part-time job. They have few skills, no plans to be retrained, nor any desire to move. Listening to the conversation, one senses they are angry, blame others for their misfortune and have no plans to better their life. A few of their friends have served time in jail and one was killed while driving intoxicated.

Unlike the group at the Legion, these young men had less than three years of employment at the plant and insufficient time to develop a middle-class lifestyle or safety net. What is totally missing from this table is hope. As for the future, they will go to the diner tomorrow, order a few beers and continue the conversation of them against the world. (Any time you come across someone that believes it is them against the world - bet the world.) These young men still have a chance to improve their lot in life, but then again, why bother. They are in a cultural prison. They believe it is too late to upgrade their skills as they are in their early thirties and are not prepared to move to an area where there are better employment prospects. Their friends are staying in this small town and they do not receive any encouragement or support to better themselves.

One important difference between the group at the diner and the other friends having lunch is middle-class values. The men at the diner do not believe that hard work is the key to success. Some live by the motto that we pretend to work and the employer pretends to pay us. They think the system is rigged and politicians do not represent their views. They believe their future is not bright and perhaps there is no reason to disagree with them.

The Bottom Line – Boomers were born into the world that minimal effort could produce a financially secure lifestyle. However, the playing field has tilted and there is greater competition for fewer opportunities. In the boomer's day, success was available regardless of the circumstances of their parents.

CHAPTER TWO

HISTORY OF WORKING FAMILIES

Nothing is more common than the desire to be uncommon

The middle class was at its peak from about 1960 to around 1990 and then started to decline. To understand why this peak was reached, it is important to understand the history of working men. Leaving out the details, which would fill a million textbooks, the history of western civilization can be summarized as follows:

- After Christ died, the Roman Empire was supreme and it ruled for a few centuries.
- Popes and kings shared power and the Catholic Church had a monopoly on education and science. As a result, nothing important happened for about a thousand years.
- Around the year 1500, explorers started heading out to the New World.
- The scientific revolution and the Renaissance ended the Church's monopoly on thought. Education and independent thinking shone light where once there was darkness.

- The industrial revolution increased employment opportunities as young men moved from farms to the cities.
- The incredible demand for consumer products following the Second World War resulted in a massive expansion of the manufacturing sector. This became the foundation for the middle class and created the opportunity for a generation of boomers to be successful.

During the last two thousand years, there were kings and queens, wars, revolutions and boundaries between countries continue to change. History classes taught us important names, who won the wars and how our country became an independent nation. Today there is a belief that the top 1% controls most of the global wealth. However, for the 2000 years following the death of Jesus, it was not the 1% that controlled the wealth; rather it was more like the top .00001%. Kings and queens mastered trickle-down economics to support an aristocracy. Many societies had a merchant class, but it was a very small segment of the population. People were extremely poor and often lived in squalor in cities or starving in the countryside. Imagine the life of peasants which made up the vast majority of society. For the most part, they are ignored in our history books as there was no reason to document their lifestyle which was slightly short of a living hell. Survival was a struggle, conscription was commonplace, diseases were often untreated, women died in childbirth and the powerful took what they wanted without repercussions.

There are two types of poor in today's world which can be simplistically classified as American poor and global poor. American poor may include families who live below the poverty line but own a smartphone. Putting food on the table is a challenge for many families, but very few die of starvation. As for the global poor, disease and famine are commonplace and digging through garbage may provide the only food for the day. Women may walk for miles to get fresh water for their family. For most of recorded time, most people met the definition of global poor.

The English philosopher Thomas Hobbes had described life before the imaginary social contract came into existence and his comments applied to most individuals before the twentieth century. He said that men lived in continual fear and danger of violent death. The life of man was solitary, poor, nasty, brutish and short.

Life was about survival, gathering food and protecting one's family. Day-to-day living was a challenge. There was no electricity, medical help, law enforcement, sewage systems, running water, or toilet paper. It was a world where the biggest and strongest just took what they wanted. If the life of men was horrific, the plight of women was significantly worse.

The industrial revolution created manufacturing jobs using newly invented machinery. Massive amounts of money were being spent on city infrastructure. Young men moved from the farm to the cities and Europe provided a wave of immigrants in search of a better life. However, the pay was low, the hours long and worker safety was an afterthought.

In the first half of the twentieth century, a number of factors came together to create a more stable life for families. This includes the seeds planted by a demographic force that has been called the greatest generation. This group consists of those born in the first 25 years of the twentieth century and many of these men fought in the Second World War. They realized by working hard; they could provide a better life for their family than the one their parents experienced. The boomers were the first generation where children were not expected to work to supplement the family income.

It was the work of unions demanding better working conditions; governments developing a social safety net and a world war that created enormous demand that acted as a perfect storm to create our middle class. Upon their return from the war, soldiers wanted wives and families and there was an enormous spike in births and consumer demand. Babies started to arrive and arrive and arrive. Perhaps the greatest advantage enjoyed by boomers was that their chance for success in life was no longer directly related to their parent's situation. In other words, the circumstances of their birth would not determine whether or not they would be successful. After the war, factories were busy as returning soldiers wanted homes, cars, furniture and big boy toys. This incredible increase in consumer demand lasted for decades. Consider the following:

- Workers with a basic education who entered the workforce in the 1960s could expect to earn more than their parents. Good luck with that in today's world.

- An immigrant who arrived in our country in the 1950s and spoke minimal English could watch his children attend university and become doctors and lawyers.

- Post-secondary school education was affordable, admission standards were not excessive and there were full-time jobs for almost everyone who graduated.

- Women and minorities had not taken their rightful place in the workforce. Once the pill was invented and barriers were starting to be reduced, a wave of talented women was unleashed on the workforce. Whereas some university classes had only a few women in the 1960s, many of today's graduating classes have a majority of female students. This may have reduced opportunities for white males, but they had better learn to suck it up since their period of dominance was coming to an end.

- Our economy had not yet enjoyed the "advantages" of free trade and globalization. Imported products were often of poor quality and could not compete with homegrown products. In the 1960s most imported Japanese products were crap. As a result, factories were hiring and if a man wanted a job, he could find employment. This was before American consultants moved to Japan and taught the importance of quality. Within a few decades, the Far East was producing high-quality products that were valued by consumers. This resulted in North American companies facing powerful global competitors who were gaining market share.

- A family could be raised on one income and children were reared by family members, rather than paid professionals.

- Although it may not have been apparent at the time, housing prices were reasonable and home ownership became a future source of wealth.

- Cradle to grave employment was common and there was a sense of loyalty to employers. Workers talked about a family-like atmosphere as part of the corporate culture. That era has been replaced with concepts such as lean and mean and job churning where individuals can expect to work for multiple employers throughout their career. This makes saving difficult as there are periods of unemployment and it is difficult to obtain sufficient service time to generate adequate pension benefits.

- Jobs were primarily full-time and those with part-time employment were often students or mothers working a few hours a week to earn extra income. The concept of full-time employment has not yet been augmented by contract staff, agents, permanent part-time and forced self-employment.

We can look nostalgically at the world the boomers inherited as no generation ever had such opportunities to find their way in life. Upon completion of high school, teenagers were expected to leave home and either get a job or go to school. It was common for those fresh out of high school to have multiple roommates and they all held jobs. Many experimented with drugs; had more sex with multiple partners and listened to music that was probably inspired by the devil.

The development of a strong middle class may be among the most important events in history. It is the catalyst for a strong economy and provides a powerful check on special interests, especially politicians. If the goal of every person is to write a story of a life with themselves as the hero, a generation was provided with opportunities that were only available to the wealthy in previous centuries. They were able to provide for their families and had the option of choosing multiple paths for their journey through life. Many were able to grow old in a secure retirement while watching their children live a happy and successful life. What happens if the middle class starts to shrink? Their spending drives the economy and if they can no longer afford to spend their income on goods and services, the cutbacks will be felt throughout the country. Henry Ford realized over a century ago that if he wanted people to purchase his automobiles, they had to be paid a reasonable salary.

Bottom Line - We understand there are enormous problems facing the world including reducing poverty, stopping the effects of climate change, solving the refugee issues and working for global peace. However, if we do not reverse the decline in the number of families able to enjoy a middle-class lifestyle, our future will be negatively impacted beyond our imagination. Increasing the size of the middle class may be the most important issue facing the next generation. It is unclear how many recognize the importance or the near impossibility of this task.

CHAPTER THREE

THE SECRET FORMULA

One can only achieve success if there is opportunity

A farmer had puppies for sale and three men answered the ad and arrived at his farm at 10:00 am on a Saturday morning. The first man drove a beat-up truck and lived in a trailer park. He has not worked in years and wanted a dog for security. It was his intention to tie the dog to a ten-foot chain and keep the dog outside the trailer. It was his depraved view that if a dog is beaten, it becomes more ferocious and a better watchdog. The second purchaser was a farmer who wanted a dog to live in the barn and provide security by keeping wild animals away from the livestock. The dog would be fed once a day and would never be allowed in the house; he was an animal after all. The third owner was a doctor who wanted a pet for his children. The new dog would eat quality food, see the vet regularly and be treated as a member of the family.

Each of the buyers reached into the cage and took a puppy. The selection process appeared random. The farmer is paid and the puppies are driven to their new homes and will never see each other again. As they leave the farm, they have no understanding of the differences in their future lifestyles, as one dog will be treated like a princess while the other two will face more hardships. One puppy was randomly chosen by the doctor and it could have just as easy been one of her sisters. Just like dogs, people are born into a set of circumstances that will impact the path they follow in life. Consider the boomers to be similar to the puppy selected by the doctor, as they were born into a world with more opportunities for success than any generation in history.

People that came of age in the 1950s and 1960s were presented with a formula that offered a higher probability of financial success as compared to those who followed a different path. There is no issue that an individual's work ethic and skills will impact the ultimate level of success to be achieved, but many naively believe they are totally responsible for their achievements. What is the formula that so many boomers followed yet did not know of its existence? The first step was to win the genetic lottery. If two children are born at the same time, in an ideal world, they would have a similar chance for success, but the earth is not one of those ideal worlds. Consider the situation of two children who are born at the same time. One is the tenth child of a single mother in a small village in Bangladesh. Feeding the family is a challenge, clean water is a luxury and a university education is not even a dream. The other child is a healthy baby born to Bill and Melinda Gates. It is possible the tenth child of the mother from Bangladesh will achieve great success, but the playing field is not level. In fact, it is so tilted that the baby's chance of achieving financial success is remote and that assumes he lives past his third birthday.

Winning the genetic lottery does not mean success is guaranteed, rather they have a higher probability of success that those who don't share their situation. Babies born in the 1950s or 60s were the winners of the genetic lottery if they were born under the following circumstances:

- Born in a democracy that respects the rule of law and rights of the individual
- A healthy baby without a learning disability
- Born into a two-parent family with both parents involved in raising the child in a loving and supportive environment
- The family does not suffer from alcoholism, drug abuse, or severe mental health issues
- The child is white and male

Being white and male were important success factors in this period. Although there is no authoritative data to back the following statement, it would not be surprising that children born today may have a greater chance of success if they met the first four criteria and were born female. This may not be true for young women born into families with religious or cultural mores that restrict her opportunities.

Decisions made in our teens set in motion a series of events that define our future. The boomer's formula for success had three different paths:

The Higher Education Option

This path was followed by many successful boomers who have retired and are enjoying a financially secure lifestyle.

- Get a university degree. The field of study was not important as there were jobs for every graduate, whether it was a degree in business or the study of English poets.
- Either become an entrepreneur or work for a top-tier employer that provided benefits and opportunities for advancement.

- Don't jump jobs. Working for two or three employers is ideal. There is an exception for individuals whose objective is to be a CEO or senior VP.
- Have a moral compass and strong work ethic.
- Purchase a home early in their career.

The Blue-Collar Option

Young men who did not choose the higher education option could have a financially secure future if they made one of the following choices:

- Get a union job in a factory
- Take an apprenticeship and master a trade
- Become an entrepreneur
- Career as a police officer or firefighter

This formula worked best for those born in the first half the boomer's generation. Those born in the late 50s and early 60s had a greater chance of facing plant closures late in their career.

A Path for Young Women

University was not an option for many women, but those following this route had a tremendous head start. Those that did not attend university could attain a secure lifestyle by:

- Becoming a nurse or a teacher
- Marrying well

In addition to selecting one of these paths, it was important to avoid the negative impact of potentially bad decisions made by teenagers. These include:

- Doing something stupid that results in a criminal record
- Developing an addiction to drugs or alcohol
- Becoming a parent as a teenager

There were outliers who found success by following a different path, but these formulae allowed the majority of boomers to achieve a higher level of financial security than any generation that preceded them.

Large companies that hired boomers had three significant advantages over companies that operate in today's competitive environment. There were very few disruptive technologies eliminating jobs, most imports were poor quality and there were very few world class global competitors. When companies were growing at an accelerated rate, there was more hiring, promotions and usually more cash. Boomers were hired at a time of economic expansion, whereas today's job market is much more challenging.

Bottom Line - For retired boomers that followed the university path and worked their entire career for a top-tier employer, it would be more common than not to retire as millionaires. This assumes they purchased a home and were not subject to divorce, illness or some rare financial calamity. It was a wonderful formula, get a post-secondary education, work for a large company, have a strong work ethic, not be beset by bad luck and retire a millionaire. They should thank their lucky stars for good decisions made as a teenager, defined benefit pension plans and being born at an ideal time in history.

CHAPTER FOUR

THE BOOMER'S APOCALYPTIC LEGACY

When it is you against the world, bet the world

Visitors to our national parks understand the importance of leaving it in the same condition as when they entered. They are a treasure for future generations and we have a duty to preserve and protect their natural beauty. This concept is easy to apply to the environment, but little thought is given to whether one generation owes any responsibility or economic legacy to those that follow. This is known as intergenerational equity. In addition to creating a strong and prosperous middle class, boomers had many magnificent accomplishments including advancements in health care, technology and food production. However, they have left many unresolved issues.

The boomer's legacy was not a conspiracy to leave problems for future generations, rather too many individuals, politicians and businesses looked out for their interests and those few voices who spoke out concerning future issues were largely ignored. The negative impact of the boomer's generation can be categorized into three legacy issues:

1. They have left a mountain of unpaid bills for future generations. This includes both government debt and the pension liabilities of civil servants.
2. As boomers move through the health care system and into retirement homes, the costs to care for this demographic spike will be enormous.
3. The environment has been ravaged in the name of economic growth and the resulting costs will be massive.

Government Debt - There were significant deficits during the Great Depression and World War Two, but previously large deficits were not common. When the boomers entered the world, government spending resulted in mild swings between modest deficits and surpluses. However, there was a major change during the boomer era as they paid insufficient taxes to fund the services they demanded. Despite ongoing deficits, there was underspending on infrastructure resulting in many of our roads, airports and bridges being dated and decaying. Future generations will inherit the financial mess of their parents and interest payments on the debt will become an increasing government expenditure. This problem will be magnified if interest rates rise in the future. Money that could have been used on education and health care will instead pay for interest and debt reduction. This is the classic definition of mortgaging the future.

In addition to debt resulting from spending exceeding tax revenue, there are also the underfunded pension liabilities of government employees. This issue is extremely important, but is very technical (boring) and does not receive the public scrutiny it deserves. The most significant problem is the methodology used by governments to calculate future pension liabilities. Since pension payments are many years in the future, a discount rate is used to calculate the current liability. A lower discount rate results in a higher liability. It would make sense the private and public sectors use the same formula to determine their pension liability, but such is not the case. The private sector is required to use a rate determined by corporate bond yields, whereas public sector pensions are allowed to use the expected rate of return on their investments. Since they assume higher rates of return than bond yields used by the private sector, their pension liability is understated. It may encourage administrators of public service pensions to select higher risk investments. This may reduce the potential liability, but if the returns do not materialize it makes a bad situation worse. Thus, a private and public sector pension could be identical in every respect, but the government's accounting methodology allows them to calculate a lower liability. The eventual payout to retired civil servants will be a combination of employee and employer contributions, investment income and possibly general tax revenue. Most private sector employers have moved away from defined benefit pension plans, especially for new employees, due to the cost of funding these plans. There is an incredible risk if equity markets go south and the employer has to make up the funding shortfall. Governments continue to maintain these plans for their employees since cost control and good governance are talking points for elections rather than a way of life.

Stockton California and Detroit Michigan declared bankruptcy and a key issue in both cities was pension liabilities. They could not meet their obligations and some court cases raised the issue of whether or not the pensions of former civil servants should be protected in bankruptcy. Perhaps the cities made promises they could not fulfill or offered excessive pension benefits in exchange for lower wages. Regardless of the reasons for offering pensions they could not afford, it is scandalous that hard-working civil servants were promised a level of retirement payments, but may eventually discover they will not receive the amounts promised.

How big an issue are two sets of accounting rules? As at December 31, 2015, public service pensions in the United States were approximately 75% funded. If they were forced to use the rules required of the private sector, these pensions would be under 50% funded. The obvious solution would be one set of rules for everyone, but such a change would result in governments reporting a greater pension liability. An upward adjustment of unfunded pension obligations will result in a call for increased cash infusions which may make sense from an economic perspective, but politically there may be more important priorities than funding civil servant pensions. Don't be surprised if there are more pension defaults if the stock market enters a long bear market. Trusting employers to pay the pension benefits they promised is the foundation of an individual's retirement.

A simple solution is to let the light shine where once there was darkness. Both private and public pensions should use the same accounting rules and all pensions could be required to make an annual public report as to the amount of their unfunded liability. This information would advise members if their pension will have issues meeting its payout obligations.

Politicians focus on the annual deficit, rather than the accumulated debt since it appears to be a more manageable issue. However, if they were accountable for the total debt plus the unfunded pension liabilities, their excuses for non-action would sound hollow. If there is no action to reduce this accumulated debt, it will fall on future taxpayers to fund.

Ongoing Boomer Expenses - Boomers are entering retirement and will transition to senior's homes and graveyards. The costs of caring for this dying generation will be enormous. This is the result of massive numbers of boomers retiring and the demand for beds, personal care workers and health care resources will exceed the supply as these geriatrics ride into the sunset. They are living longer which results in an extended period to receive government pensions and possibly longer times in chronic care rooms when they are no longer able to look after themselves. There is an opportunity to move towards greater utilization of a user pay system, but this idea has not gained traction.

In addition to the health care crisis, our aging infrastructure is problematic. Construction spending is a common stimulus for governments to address the issue of a slowing economy. However, future generations must not only continue spending on roads, bridges and sewer systems to meet their growth requirements, but they must fix an aging infrastructure that was not adequately addressed during the period when boomers controlled the government.

Environment and Climate Change - Boomers demanded economic growth despite the negative impact on the environment. These issues could have been addressed, but at the cost of a slowdown in the economy and this was not a priority for my generation. Natural resources have been depleted, the environment damaged and many species of animals are gone forever. Weather is becoming more severe and the impact on crops and wildlife is impossible to quantify. Sea levels are rising, the earth's atmosphere is getting hotter, there are more wildfires and water management will become a critical issue. The consequences of climate change are severe and it appears that it is going to get worse before it has a chance of getting better. Is it possible to take action against climate change without restricting economic output? As a society, we are challenged to reach a consensus on this issue.

Perhaps the saddest component of the boomer's legacy is that for the past hundred years, every generation has been financially better off than their parents. The boomers may have ended the streak and left their children to pay the bill. It is possible the younger generation may attempt to have the boomers pay for their legacy before they leave this planet forever. For example, governments could increase wealth and estate taxes or make boomers pay the full cost of health care during their extended retirement period. There is probably no political will to go after the boomers to pay these expenses, plus that generation votes in higher proportions than their children and they control an enormous amount of wealth and political power.

As large numbers of boomers retire, conventional thinking suggests that it will create a vast number of employment opportunities for younger workers. However, the replacement process will not hire a new worker for everyone that retires. Technological advancements and "right sizing" results in many employees not being replaced. Perhaps most disheartening is the nature of the jobs that will be offered to new hires. When employees retire, they may have been members of defined benefit pension plans and had a certain level of benefits. Odds are the replacement worker will not be offered the same level of pensions. As full-time employees depart, replacements may be contract workers earning a significantly lower salary, have minimal benefits and no job security.

Many believe that the demise of the middle class could result in the death of democracy as it is practiced today. The disadvantaged may seek the solutions of radical politicians which may range from idealistically naïve to the downright dangerous. If change through the ballot box is considered too slow or ineffective, some may take to the streets. A strong middle class is crucial for democracy and our economy, yet we are watching it shrink and our government appears to be at a loss how to reverse the slide. It may be an issue during election campaigns, as our politicians will have a plan to restore the middle class. They always have a plan. How are these plans from all of our recent elections working so far?

Perhaps the biggest difference between the world the boomers entered and the one they will leave behind is the inequality of opportunity for our youth. The boomers were presented with unlimited opportunities and the circumstances of their birth did not restrict their potential. Whether they were born a carpenter's son, children from a family who just emigrated from Italy and spoke little English or a doctor's daughter, university was available to almost everyone and graduates that selected that path were able to enjoy success on many levels. The world has changed. Although almost everyone may have the potential to attend university, the playing field has tilted in favor of high-income families. Their children have the following advantages as compared to those from the working poor:

- They attend great schools in fine neighborhoods.
- The parents can provide financial support to overcome challenges on their academic journey, such as tutoring.
- Higher education has become expensive and wealthy families can eliminate cost as a barrier.
- Children from low-income families may face obstacles at home that can inhibit their ability to perform well in school.
- Children from high-income families are more likely to have two parents involved in their life and one or more of these parents may have a post-secondary education. These families value education and as parents, they operate on the assumption their children will attend university. This environment has a positive impact on their children's ability to succeed in school.

- This final point is certainly not a universal truth as there are so many exceptions that many doubt its applicability. If a child has two parents that have completed university, they may have a higher IQ than the average and this may give their children a genetic advantage. This raises the nature vs. nurture argument. However, there are so many gifted children that come from lower-income families; it is difficult to generalize. However, if one child has two parents that have both completed their Ph.D. and a second is from a single mom who works in a fast food restaurant, both children may achieve incredible success, but the former child may have an easier road.

The pendulum has swung back. Before the arrival of boomers, children from wealthy families entered life with significant advantages. That changed with the baby boomer's generation as there were so many opportunities for success that their path in life was not restricted by the circumstances of their birth. We are reverting to a world where children from financially successful two-parent families have a higher probability of a successful career. Everything that is old is new again.

Bottom Line - As boomers move to retirement homes and into the great beyond, they have left two types of legacies. On an individual level, this generation has accumulated incredible wealth which will be transferred to their beneficiaries. However collectively, the most privileged generation in history has left behind a world that will cause future governments to spend too much time, effort and financial resources attempting to clean up issues that were left unresolved.

If boomers could have resolved two issues, their children's future would have been brighter. Eliminating the accumulated debt and addressing the climate change issue would have laid the groundwork for our children and grandchildren to take charge of their collective destiny. Unfortunately, that was beyond the skill set of my generation.

CHAPTER FIVE

UNDERCLASS

Show me your friends at age nineteen and I can tell the story of the rest of your life

The term underclass refers to those at the bottom of the economic ladder, often living near or below the poverty line. It includes the elderly, the mentally and physically disabled, the long-term unemployed and those that refuse to work. It is a mistake to paint this group with one broad brush and apply stereotypes such as welfare bums, white trash or rednecks. It is simplistic and wrong.

The underclass can be broken into four broad groupings, which will be called quadrants. It is difficult to measure their specific makeup as there can be significant overlap between the groups. The quadrants are:

Quadrant One - Opportunity Lost

This group is comprised of individuals that struggle to support their family because they lack opportunities for suitable employment. They are the working poor who may lack skills or an education but have the desire for full-time employment. Many were formerly classed as working families or blue-collar workers, but they encountered unfortunate circumstances such as a factory closing. It may include single mothers who would be willing to work, but after paying child care expenses, the resulting low take-home pay makes the decision to stay home a reasonable option. Some were financially secure in their old country, but immigrating did not work out as intended. It is possible to be a doctor before emigrating and a cab driver in their new home. This quadrant may also include families that suffered through serious illness, bankruptcy, or divorce.

Quadrant Two - Unable to Work

It consists of individuals that are legitimately unable to work, often because of age or disability. There is almost no chance they will ever become self-sufficient. They rely on government assistance and it may be their only source of income.

Quadrant Three - Intergenerational Poverty

Some families live in poverty just as their parents and grandparents lived in similar circumstances. They may live in isolated communities, or there may be cultural or language issues that restrict integrating into the rest of society. Immigrants, both legal and illegal, are often members of this subset. It would appear that mobility would resolve many of the issues, but cultural ties are often too strong.

Quadrant Four - Bums, Slackers and Criminals

The final group consists of those who do not want to work and will game the system to their advantage. They often share the belief that work is for suckers. They may have bad backs and receive disability payments as it pays more than unemployment insurance and lasts longer. One of the unintended consequences of receiving disability payments is that in some jurisdictions it leads to qualifying for a medical marijuana license. Talk about killing two birds with one stone. They may receive various forms of government assistance, engage in criminal activity or earn income that is not reported to the government.

One of the important differentiators of the first quadrant from the rest of the underclass is work ethic and values. They want a job and the opportunity to provide for their family. Despite their current circumstances, these families still consider themselves as middle class. Many maintain a modest lifestyle if both spouses are employed. However, living pay day to pay day means they are one crisis short of being unable to pay the bills. A lack of income does not destroy the values that have been built up over a lifetime. They understand that life has dealt them a major hurt, but it does not change who they are.

In the remaining quadrants, some are unable to work, but a significant number lack the desire for full-time employment. They may show up late, disobey direction and only work sufficient hours to qualify for government benefits. Too many live in a culture that does not promote social mobility or bettering themselves. They live as their parents lived and probably assume their children will adopt the same lifestyle. Some will use educational opportunities to advance, but many will never leave their community. Young people with the intelligence to succeed often lack the motivation to leave or do not have the family support that encourages them to follow their dreams. Those who talk of leaving may be considered as "too big for their britches."

In the 1960s, many small towns had a major employer, such as a mine, mill or factory and often the town grew around that company. Supporting industries were established such as retail, banking and law enforcement. Then over the next few decades, many of the large employers closed or moved away. The skilled and better educated often left in search of employment elsewhere, but for those who stayed, the prospects for reasonable paying jobs was poor. When the plant closes and the skilled workers leave, the result is often long-term poverty and reduced expectations. The exodus of jobs is detrimental to the town's tax base. Despite their parent's circumstances, children have the option of following the educational highway to a better life. Unfortunately, in many small towns and neighborhoods in large cities with a high degree of poverty, there is higher participation in the drug culture, higher levels of addiction, teenage pregnancy and lower rates of high school graduation. Sometimes it takes a teacher, a coach, or a parent that can describe a future that is beyond the narrow horizon of their life and motivate a child to pursue a higher education and a chance at a better life.

The size of the underclass is growing at an alarming rate. This group is often referred to in a condescending manner by the press and politicians as a group that needs our help. Any suggestion of better than thou or pity totally misses the point of this group. It is true they are not in a good place, but the question is how they got there and what can be done to provide the opportunity to move up the economic ladder. Many people who are categorized as members of the underclass can identify with the following:

- They made some incredibly stupid decisions as teenagers and many lacked the support system to get past this error. Screwing up as a teenager is more of a rite of passage than an exception.
- Opportunities that were available to boomers have disappeared as a result of free trade deals, technological advancements and plant closings. Free trade has many winners, but for many industries in small towns, it is an economic blow from which there is no recovery.
- They were born into a dysfunctional low-income, single-parent family, or a home with two adults

who are dealing with drugs, alcohol, or domestic abuse issues. A lack of two loving parents involved in a child's life can create barriers that many cannot rise above. There is often a lack of parental encouragement to acquire skills or pursue an education. It can be too great a price to pay to leave their friends and family in search of a better life.

Middle-class values are underrepresented in the third and fourth quadrants. With the loss of income comes a lack of options and it easy to lose hope for a better future. It can be a contributor to failed marriages, which can result in a less stable family which may further restrict a child's opportunity for a better life. Former breadwinners may feel a total loss of control and believe their decisions no longer matter. Social mobility is tough enough when people lose their source of employment; it is near impossible when all hope has been killed and the family is falling apart.

One of the fundamental differences between the middle class and the third and fourth quadrants is the answer to the question of whether or not they know anyone who has served time in jail. Many middle-class families would answer in the negative, whereas the opposite answer would be a common response from the bottom two quadrants. Criminals are more likely to come from the underclass except the opportunity lost quadrant. These families retain their values, but there are certain risks if they are pushed out of middle-class neighborhoods by forces beyond their control and relocate to more affordable housing. Their children may befriend some bad kids who do not share the values of friends from their former neighborhood. Perhaps there is less ambition, or the kids have more time on their hands and less parental supervision. This is when bad things can happen. Many children introduced to this environment keep their old friends, stay in sports and are wise enough to stay on the high road. However, some will find trouble and this may impact the child's ability to use the available educational pathways to rejoin the middle class as an adult. It is not low income that is a driver of crime; rather there is a strong correlation between violence and neighborhoods that have a higher incidence of alcoholism, drug use, single-parent households and high unemployment.

There is an economic term known as the dependency ratio which is not widely used outside of academic circles. It is the ratio of dependants (children plus seniors) as a percentage of the entire population. An increasing ratio has serious consequences for a country as government spending on education, health care and pensions are primarily aimed at this group. If the percentage of dependants is increasing, then the size of the workforce that pays taxes is decreasing. As boomers retire, there will be increasing pressure on overtaxed workers to support their health care costs and government pensions. The bottom line is that a smaller percentage of the population is paying taxes, while a growing segment is receiving benefits. That suggests either higher tax rates or larger deficits. There is an alternate fable that arises in election years. The government will be able to reduce taxes and lower the debt due to increased efficiencies in government operations and higher than forecasted economic growth.

If a neighborhood consists of families on government assistance, it tends to have poorer schools. A lack of family finances can restrict the children's opportunity for extra-curricular activities such as sports. The impact on families as they are pushed out of the middle class is more than a reduction of lifestyle due to lost family income. There is a human cost that we may never fully understand, cannot measure and are unsure of the impact on each member of the family.

One interesting observation on the difference between the underclass and higher-income families came from a school employee who visited different educational institutions in the city on a regular basis. By standing in the parking lot waiting for mothers to pick up their young children after school, she said there are recurring differences between the mothers from high-income families compared to those in the economically disadvantaged neighborhoods. These generalizations are:

- The quality of the car is an obvious difference as higher-income families can afford more expensive vehicles.
- The average mom from a poorer neighborhood was typically heavier than upper-income moms.
- The wealthier moms were significantly better dressed.
- The moms from the better schools were typically in their early thirties as compared to the other moms who were in the range of seventeen to twenty-two years of age.
- The mothers from economically disadvantaged areas were more likely to have visible tattoos and less likely to be wearing a wedding ring. This latter observation was confirmed as she interacted with the families.

These anecdotal observations have no implications for determining who is a better mother, but it does reinforce the view of "two Americas." This expression became famous when John Edwards was running for President in 2004 and spoke of a society that could be divided between the haves and the have-nots. Many members of the underclass require some dependency strategy to survive. A lack of money, when combined with an absence of discipline, makes self-sufficiency an ongoing struggle and they are often dependent on the government or a partner for day-to-day survival.

Bottom Line – It is easy to measure the economic impact of a lack of opportunity among the underclass, but there is a human cost of living in poverty in one of the richest countries in the world. We try to resolve the issue by throwing boatloads of money at those in need of assistance, but we have been unable to create opportunities to build self-sufficiency.

CHAPTER SIX

PAIN OF BLUE-COLLAR WORKERS

*Other people may be smarter, but there is
no excuse for letting them outwork you*

When older white men reminisce about the past, it has been suggested those favoring the "Leave it to Beaver" world of the 1950s tend to be conservative in their politics, whereas those who prefer the free love and social justice decade of the 1960s take a more liberal perspective. The 1950s was the decade when the white male was at the peak of his power and influence. The pent-up demand after World War Two resulted in jobs that paid a sufficient salary to purchase a house and raise a family. As for education, completing high school was ideal, but not necessary. There were a few exceptions, but white men ran the government, corporations, hospitals and religious organizations. At this time in our history, men were afforded many advantages, simply by being male.

That world has faded away and it has been replaced by an economy where a man with just a high school education is often underemployed since well-paying jobs emphasize brain over brawn. Technology has reduced the need for muscle in the workplace. Many men without a college education often lack job security and are angry about their position in the world. Statistics suggest that

41

many poorly educated males have dropped out of the labor market, which raises the question as to how do they support themselves. The answer is females, family and the government. No hope, little money and too much time on their hands, what could go wrong?

In addition to workplace issues, statistics suggest that this group will have more difficulty finding a spouse and should they get married; the probability of staying together in a happy relationship is decreasing. It is intuitive that a lack of education will have ramifications in the job market, but why will it be tougher to have a happy marriage? Let's be very clear, some of these young men will find a wonderful spouse, raise great children and have a very satisfying life. However, the probability of this occurring will continue to decrease.

To understand this phenomenon, look at these men through the eyes of a woman. When the boomer's parents were selecting mates, pregnancy was the easy path to marriage. A woman who found herself pregnant in 1960 and did not want to marry the father of her child had options, most of them bad. She could raise the child as a single mother in a period when few women had full-time jobs. Providing for her child would be problematic unless there was financial support from either the father of the child or her family, plus she faced a significant social stigma. If being a single parent was not an acceptable option, she could give the child up for adoption or do the honorable thing and marry the father. For many families it was a basic rule, getting pregnant meant getting married. Many young women were taught that the rhythm method was an effective birth control technique, which is one of the reasons why many teenagers became mothers.

How did young women who were not pregnant choose their mates? In addition to obvious considerations such as common interests, physical attraction and friendship, many women wanted to find a spouse who could support her financially and be a kind and loving father. This ideal mate was often a physically fit young man who had a high school education and may have followed in his father's footsteps at the local factory. From the female perspective, this type of husband would provide the family income she desired or at least the lifestyle enjoyed by most of her friends.

Let's move forward a few decades and look at the considerations of today's young women as they consider a potential spouse. Not only do many women have a post-secondary school education, but they are graduating at higher rates than white males. When their fathers went to university, there may have been a few women in their class, whereas now it is not unusual to have females as the majority of many graduating classes. Outside of senior positions in most religions, there are very few vocations that women are not mastering and may soon dominate. Educated women not only challenge the conventions of their parents and grandparents, but they have smashed the stereotypes. For example:

- In the 1960s, it was common to be married by the age of twenty-two. By age thirty, terms like old maid were being whispered. Today women may marry later in life as they establish their career, should they decide that marriage is a good fit for their lifestyle.
- Unlike her grandmother who needed a man to provide financial security, today's young ladies are more than capable of taking care of themselves. The financial status of a potential spouse may still be important, but he may supplement the family income, rather than be the primary bread winner.

The stereotypes of females from bygone times have been blown away. When today's woman chooses a mate, a high school graduate who may have been the ideal catch in 1961 may be unacceptable by today's standards. There are exceptions, but many women with post-secondary education are looking for partners with a similar background. If the goal is predicting how well a child will do in school, there is a strong correlation between the child's success and the parent's level of education. Not only does the parent's experience value an education, but they have the financial resources to assist their children on their academic journey. Another trend is that higher-income couples have lower divorce rates than those at the other end of the economic spectrum. Two parents involved in a child's life is an important factor in their academic and personal growth. Financially secure families tend to live in better neighborhoods with great schools which may reduce the number of negative factors that can inhibit a child's education and development. This does not suggest that a child from a low-income, single-parent family living in a rough neighborhood cannot be successful in school, it is just the odds are longer. Bill Clinton and Barack Obama did not have a typical two family parenting situation, but both had reasonable success in life. So where does this leave today's underemployed male that has a high school diploma or less? The pool of potential spouses is much smaller and a perceived inability to provide a financially stable income will place these men lower in the food chain as potential mates. Many women with only a high school background may seek financial security in a potential spouse, so the high school graduate may not be her first choice.

Two of the biggest factors impacting employment have been free trade and technology. If the manufacturing process was labor intensive, jobs were often moved offshore in search of cheaper wages. If the process was capital intensive, investments were made in technology. As a result, the need for low-skilled workers plummeted. Companies can manufacture products with fewer employees and computers allow more output with less staff. New opportunities have opened up in areas of technology, but laid off workers may not have the skills or the aptitude to take these jobs. Automobile manufacturers require fewer workers and although technology firms are hiring, it is rare, if not impossible, to be downsized at General Motors and have the skill set to work at Google. Even if the government provides financing for a six-month retraining course in technology, they will not be on the radar of the big tech companies.

Underemployed males are disappearing from our national statistics. Their labor participation rate is significantly lower than other men and many live in poverty. It appears that for every unemployed white male looking for a job, many have no interest in finding full-time employment. They survive by a combination of welfare, disability insurance, financial support from a girlfriend or unreported income, which may or may not be legally earned. One government stat indicates that over 50% of nonworking males are receiving disability payments. Over a third of these men live in poverty and the majority does not have a wife. There is a county in Arkansas where over 10% of the working-age adults receive disability payments. Needless to say, this county has been hit hard by plant closings.

The chapter addressed the issues of the pain of the blue-collar worker and it was intended to discuss the mental anguish of this important group. However, evidence suggests that the pain is also physical. Underemployed white working men tend to have poorer health and increased death rates compared to other subsets of the population. It is a combination of obesity, drinking, suicides and the use of drugs such as fentanyl. The question is whether or not there is a strong correlation between the decline of manufacturing jobs and the health of those that were previously employed in this sector. Declining health may be another byproduct of a declining middle class. This problem is compounded if these families cannot afford medical expenses, such as prescriptions that are necessary for their recovery.

Bottom Line - Working families are the backbone of our country and we let them down. We must create opportunities for their families, or our country will have a hollowed out middle class with two distinct economic cultures - the haves and the have-nots. The friction between these two groups may not end well for either group. One of the best ways to create stress is to eliminate options. Many low-skilled and undereducated males are out of options. Sitting and do nothing is not in their nature, so we should not expect them to go quietly into the night.

CHAPTER SEVEN

WHY THE PLAYING FIELD TILTED

There is only one way to know what a customer, friend or a spouse wants, you have to ask them

There were four periods of economic modernization and the first three created opportunities and prosperity, but the fourth has been damaging for many working families. The first was the agricultural revolution. Mechanization and new technologies resulted in a phenomenal increase in food output. This was followed by the industrial revolution which utilized new machines to expand the manufacturing sector and build our country's infrastructure. This created a need for workers and most able young men who wanted work could find it with little difficulty. These jobs had long hours and low pay. The third event was the creation of a middle class following the Second World War. Boomers were born into this world of unlimited opportunity. The final phase was the technological revolution that introduced computers, robotics and artificial intelligence that requires workers to attain specialized skills.

When the boomers entered the workforce, it was a downhill path to a middle-class lifestyle. Jobs were plentiful and companies were prepared to train new hires. Many larger employers had an unwritten social contract with their employees, which often included life-long employment, a family-like atmosphere, plus a pension and benefits package. Underlying this implied social contract was a mutual commitment and loyalty by both parties. That world is either dead or dying as individuals are facing new barriers to acquiring membership in the middle class.

The playing field has tilted in the other direction. The most significant issue is the concept of sector rotation, or in layman's terms, the job market has changed. At the time when levels of manufacturing employment started to decline, there was growth in the fields of technology, health care and education, but many blue-collar workers lacked the skills to move to these jobs. The service sector experienced rapid growth with well-paying jobs in the financial services sector and lower-paying jobs in retail and the fast food industry.

Baby boomers could acquire manufacturing jobs with minimal education, training or experience. As these jobs disappeared, a new generation of lower-skilled and less educated workers struggle to compete in the new high growth sectors that require education and training.

Another obstacle to membership in the middle class is the changing makeup of the family. Traditional two-parent families are declining in the underclass. Many children from lower-income families will struggle to compete with children from more affluent households. We are entering a world that is becoming divided between the haves and the have-nots and those at the bottom have the cards stacked against them. This is not the world the boomers entered.

The middle class is expanding in the third world and it is fantastic that levels of poverty are being reduced and more people are enjoying financial security and the pleasures of consumerism. These countries are experiencing what North America and Western Europe enjoyed when the boomers entered the world. As western countries experience a disruption of their middle class, is it possible that the growth in the third world is connected to the struggle of many families in North America?

Bottom Line - There is a sense of both anger and frustration in our community. Working families are angry that plants have closed and well-paying jobs are disappearing. They understand the impact on their family and believe our political leaders are unable or unwilling to address these issues with anything but rhetoric and unfulfilled promises. Those higher up the economic ladder with a better education and secure jobs may not share their anger, but they have a sense of frustration that their children may not have the opportunities that were afforded to their generation. If everyone continues to act in their best interests, such as companies maximizing profit by moving jobs overseas, governments focusing on retaining power and powerful interests ensuring they retain their wealth, who is looking out for your family? This demographic spike that is the luckiest generation of all time has left a scorched earth policy that will limit the ability of the next generation to right the ship. Strip away opportunity, eliminate hope and the question has to be asked whether those who can no longer support themselves will sit on their hands and accept the fate they have been dealt.

The boomers had a great ride, but future generations must approach the job market with more skills than any generation before them. We are returning to a world of haves and have-nots and the schism between these groups will continue to grow. Bridging that gap may be the biggest challenge we face in the next decade.

PART TWO

THE FUTURE

Many families face an uncertain economic future. The working poor must confront many obstacles as they try to stake their claim to a middle-class lifestyle, while other families, who thought they were financially secure, will be victims of job loss and lack suitable alternative employment. This section outlines a pessimistic view of the future and explains why funding a dignified retirement may be beyond the reach of many families.

CHAPTER EIGHT

TOWARDS A BLEAK FUTURE

When you fail, fail fast, move on

Barry McGuire had a top-selling hit in the 60's called the Eve of Destruction which forecasts political instability and the very real possibility of nuclear war. Most of his fears never came to pass. Perhaps it is too easy to be pessimistic about our economic future, but it is unclear if we can agree on our problems, let alone the steps necessary to resolve the myriad of issues that we face. There are global forces and trends that are beyond our control that can do grave damage to both our nation and our family. It is uncertain if our government can protect us from these external threats. In theory, there are possible solutions to our dilemma, but we are a polarized nation and there does not appear to be a political will or consensus to address these issues. There is the possibility of some future black swan event changing the course of our future, but these are almost impossible to predict. A black swan event is something that is highly improbable and significantly deviates beyond what is normally accepted. Black Swan was a term coined by author Nassim Taleb in his excellent book on the topic.

There are some trends and issues that if remain unresolved have the potential to create turmoil and these include:

- External factors such as rogue nations, super bugs and the disenfranchised may create havoc.
- The rate of turbulence in the job market will increase as the result of technology and globalization.

Rogue Nations, Super Bugs and the Disenfranchised

Life has many risks and prudent individuals can manage many of these potential problems. Life insurance can protect a family in case of premature death. Liability insurance can safeguard assets in case of an accident and not smoking reduces the risk of disease and early death. However, regardless of what successes we have accumulated in our journey through life, we are vulnerable to external risks. Rogue nations have nuclear weapons; terrorists want to attack our country and superbugs infect our hospitals. Climate change is impacting the world, but not in a positive way. We expect our water supply, homes and streets to be safe. As individuals, we have little impact on the outside world and expect our government to address these issues.

If a poor economy results in high unemployment especially among young men, it may be reasonable to expect some level of civil strife. Not to suggest that people will take to the streets with pitchforks, but if we create a subclass with a poor education and a bleak outlook, is it unreasonable that disenfranchised will lash out? This may give rise to protests, possible violence and the growth of more extreme political parties. A weak economy has a greater impact on those at the bottom end of the economic ladder and they may choose not to suffer in silence. If and when they strike out, their pain may be shared throughout every part of our society.

In the next decade or so, the world will add another billion people which raises the question as to how are we going to feed these people and provide the necessary economic opportunities? Over the past century agricultural related technology has advanced at a greater rate than population growth and there has been much success producing sufficient food to feed the world. It is a different question if we can distribute food to those who require assistance as too many still go to bed hungry. As cities expand, we use up farmland while climate change makes it difficult to predict the impact on agricultural output. There is a somewhat inaccurate term known as the "bottom billion." Despite economic gains around the globe, more than a billion people still struggle with extreme poverty and will not have any semblance of what can be considered a normal life. The time frame to add a billion people to the planet continues to shrink. As these newborns grow into young adults with limited opportunities to share in the wealth of nations, how will these angry men and women in our country and around the world express their frustration?

The threat of terrorism goes beyond an increased likelihood of death. In North America, the attacks have been horrific, but more people have died from murder, car accidents and doctor error in hospitals. The fear of terrorism can impact society in numerous ways beyond the actual death and destruction. It can cause a negative impact on the stock market and increased government spending on counterterrorism activities, so the money is not being spent elsewhere. Productivity will suffer. Consider the number of hours people have spent in lines at airports going through security checks. Tourism may suffer and there is a greater level of insecurity among the public.

A family can make the correct decision at every point in their life, but be subject to external forces that can shatter their plans. These forces are beyond our control and we rely on the government to keep the barbarians at the gate and provide a safe environment. We trust our government is up to the task.

Technology and Globalizations Impact on Jobs

The field of economics is often subject to criticism, many of which is unfair. Some complain it is too theoretical and although it may explain what happened in the past, professionals in this field do not have a great track record of predicting future economic events. Ronald Reagan once joked that he wanted to hire a one-armed economist so he could never say "while on the other hand." One principle that most economists tend to agree is that trade and globalization create wealth. Generating more wealth is positive. Thus it follows that free trade is a concept that should be supported. The theory suggests free trade will create wealth at both the global and local levels; however, it is not equally distributed throughout society. If the major world powers are attempting to punish a rogue nation, do they place an embargo on the country or do they force it into a free trade agreement? Closed economies do not grow at the rate of open societies. In a typical free trade agreement, a country may receive the following benefits:

- Companies that export have access to new markets.
- Large companies will find it easier to build manufacturing plants overseas. The workers in these third-world countries will receive lower wages and benefits, than employees in the home country. Not only will this create additional profit for the companies, but it creates wealth overseas and pulls large segments of their society out of extreme poverty. A salary of a few dollars a day may allow breadwinners to feed their family.

- As poorer countries develop a middle class, it will create new markets for our exporters and stabilize the economy of third world countries.
- Consumers are major winners under a free trade agreement. Not only are tariffs reduced or eliminated, but the products made by those few dollars a day workers will be exported to North America and consumers will pay lower prices.
- Free trade agreements often include improving labor standards in third world countries and protecting intellectual property rights.

Free trade agreements make certain companies more profitable; consumers pay reduced prices and poverty is being reduced in the third world. This sounds great, but unfortunately, the weaknesses of these deals are often minimized by proponents of free trade. The potential losers include companies that pay their employees $30 per hour but must compete with new competition that exports products and pay their workers a few dollars per day. When employers cannot compete with foreign competition, factories close and workers lose their jobs. If the manufacturing sector continues to shrink, there are fewer opportunities to find well-paying jobs, especially for men and women who lack a post-secondary school education. As companies look for ways to meet global competitive pressures, they consider options such as outsourcing, the use of part-time staff and contract labor.

There are two arguments put forward that attempt to minimize the negatives of free trade. Firstly, increased competition can be a positive influence as it forces companies to become more productive and innovative. There is some theoretical truth to that argument, but the reality is that most companies are already productive and it is extremely difficult to compete and pay fair wages when offshore competitors pay workers a few dollars per day.

Secondly, there is an acknowledgment that workers who are displaced require retraining and a short-term safety net. This is problematic as short-term benefits expire and if manufacturing jobs continue to disappear there are more workers chasing a declining supply of jobs. Taking a twelve-month course at a community college is not realistically retraining the workers unless they can earn a living that is approximately equal to their former job. Our track record on retraining workers to acquire new skills that result in a comparable salary to their previous employment is not good.

From an academic perspective, free trade creates wealth for both companies and residents of the third world, while providing consumers with lower prices. Many people accept the argument that free trade creates wealth, but if prosperity is created in Bangladesh and the loss is closing the only factory in your hometown, do you care if there is a net global wealth gain when friends and family members lose their job?

Advancements in technology have been positive for both consumers and businesses, but it is also a disruptive force. As technology creates new jobs, it causes layoffs in other industries. Unfortunately, those displaced in the old industries seldom have the skill set to apply for the newly created jobs.

Most workers will be exposed to new technology throughout their careers. The way a job is performed today will probably change in ten years. There is a joint responsibility of both employers and employees to keep abreast of the tools that technology provides. Since employers may or may not provide the necessary training, employees that do not keep current, do so at their peril. It is not just individual jobs that will be reduced through technological innovation, but companies and entire industries will disappear. This disruption will cause significant policy issues for all levels of government. Those that are displaced from high-paying jobs because of technology will not be satisfied with a lower-paying service job. A permanent position in the underclass is not an acceptable alternative to most families.

Bottom Line - Consider all of the trends and recent developments in the global economy and it is a challenge to find any of these trends that will benefit working families. It is a meaner and more competitive world than the one inherited by the boomers. Many families will be pushed off the economic ladder and be unable to recover. We need a good dose of optimism, but that is becoming increasingly rare, especially for those who are living pay day to pay day.

CHAPTER NINE

THE FOG OF RETIREMENT

As we age, we can become ourselves

Boomers who were employed by large organizations with defined benefit pension plans tend to have financially secure retirements, whereas those without a company pension may struggle. Fast forward twenty-five years into the future when many boomers have died off and a new generation is entering retirement. There are two schools of thought concerning the number of years individuals may work in the future. One view suggests that companies may need fewer workers due to technological advancements and this will force people to retire earlier than anticipated. If this view is correct, workers will have fewer years of employment to save for retirement, plus they will have a longer period of retirement to finance. Without a defined benefit plan or a significant investment portfolio, funding a lengthy retirement will be a challenge. The converse position suggests that workers may not retire until they are in their seventies because they cannot afford to quit working. In many cases, this may be inconsistent with the needs of employers. In all likelihood, retirement will be a combination of these two views and both scenarios are potentially problematic for those involved.

Types of Pensions - To understand the retirement dilemma, it is important to differentiate the two major types of pension plans which are defined benefit and defined contribution plans. A defined benefit plan promises employees a certain level of pension payments based on some combination of years of service and final salary. For example, the pension could be calculated as 60% of the average of the employee's final five years' salary, if the individual has thirty years of service. There are multiple variations of pension formulae and the plan may be company paid or employees may make contributions. Regardless of the formula, it is the employer's responsibility to ensure there are sufficient funds to make the promised level of payments throughout the retirement period. Pension assets result from a combination of contributions, investment income and growth in asset values. Since most pension plans have a significant equity component, an increase in stock values results in a corresponding rise in the value of the pension assets. However, an extended bear market can be catastrophic.

A defined contribution pension plan makes no promises as to the amount of pension income retired employees will receive. There is a formula that determines the level of contributions. For example, employees may have a pension amount deducted that is equal to 4% of gross pay and the employer may match these contributions. Employees will normally make the investment decisions and there will be a sum of money at retirement which is used to purchase a stream of retirement income, such as an annuity. Investment decisions made by the employee, interest rates and stock values will determine the size of the pension payments to be received in retirement.

The fundamental difference between a defined contribution and defined benefit plan is who bears the investment risk. If the investments underperform, it is often the result of falling stock values. If a defined benefit plan has insufficient assets to pay the promised level of pensions, the employer is required to make additional contributions. Thus, an employee is not affected by investment losses and does not bear any investment risk. This is not the case for defined contribution plans; if the investments decline in value, the employees will receive a smaller pension.

In the 1970s, most pensions were defined benefit plans. In today's economy, except in the civil service or government regulated jobs, it is rare to find defined benefit pensions offered to new employees. Many employers often have two distinct plans, defined benefit for older employees and defined contribution plans for recent hires. Many employers are not prepared to take the investment risk if the stock market underperforms. Not only do employees with defined contribution plans normally have to make their investment decisions, but a conservative investor may allocate only a small portion of their investments to equity. Another concern is the possibility that low interest rates are the new normal. If this scenario unfolds, it will be almost impossible for employees to invest in fixed income products and generate sufficient pension income to fund their retirement.

One of the great advantages of being a member of a defined benefit pension plan is the existence of a targeted retirement date. For example, individuals that are members of a pension plan that allows retirement after 30 years of service will have a target date for retiring and an approximation of their annual pension income. Consider the case of an employee who is a member of a defined contribution plan. The amount of the final pension will be dependent upon future investments returns, which are unknown. Thus, the individual cannot select a target retirement date and be assured with any degree of certainty that the necessary funds will be available.

A defined benefit pension plan is the ideal vehicle to fund retirement. Defined contribution plans are a weaker alternative that may provide an adequate retirement income, but there are many potential pitfalls and the eventual payout is an unknown. In addition to pensions, governments have legislated various tax-assisted retirement vehicles. For example, the United States has 401(k) and IRA plans while Canada has Registered Retirement Savings Plans and Tax-Free Savings Accounts. In addition to making the appropriate investment decisions, individuals should maximize their annual contribution based upon the limits set by the government. Unfortunately, many young families either lack the cash or prioritize current consumption. These plans work best for individuals that utilize the services of an investment advisor and have a reasonable level of financial sophistication. In far too many cases, the underclass does not have the money to utilize these retirement vehicles.

I spoke with two colleagues who attended separate meetings at a major university concerning the school's defined contribution plan and other retirement options. The audience consisted of university employees and some recent graduates with advanced degrees. Both of my colleagues were flabbergasted at the lack of knowledge this supposedly intelligent group had concerning pensions, retirement and investing. If these perceived brainiacs are struggling, is it surprising the average person who has no training in these fields may be unable to develop an investment strategy to fund thirty years of retirement? It is possible that some defined contribution members will put all of their money into equity investments and the market will rise for thirty consecutive years and their pension will exceed the level of income from a defined benefit plan. If it works, it would be known as the "too stupid to fail" strategy. There are numerous pitfalls for individuals making investment decisions, but these can be minimized by selecting an appropriate financial advisor. Despite the number of qualified financial advisors that are available, many receive poor advice and the unsophisticated are often unable to judge the skill set of those providing financial input or challenge their recommendations. Some will not seek advisors as they perceive themselves as experts on almost everything. This tends to be a male characteristic. Other do-it-yourselfers may be too conservative and only invest in fixed-income investments that may never generate the necessary level of income. However, members of a defined benefit plan have world-class professionals making the investment decisions and if the investments do not meet expectations, their employers will make up the loss. There are too many opportunities for failure in defined contribution plans.

Consider the differences between the boomer's retirement and that of future generations:

- At the beginning of the twenty-first century, companies were coming to the realization they could no longer afford defined benefit pension plans. As a result, new employees were often shifted to defined contribution plans. Apparently, affordability was not an issue for many public service jobs, so they were able to maintain the status quo. The result will be a decreased proportion of retirees with defined benefit pensions and increased poverty among seniors.
- As workers realize the amount of money required to fund their retirement, it may result in a delayed retirement as individuals need additional years of service to increase their pension benefits. This work extension will also provide a few more years to increase savings and reduce any outstanding debts.
- Advancements in health care will extend life expectancy. This results in a longer retirement

and increased opportunities for seniors to outlive their money. If an extended life only prolongs the number of years a senior is living with dementia or Alzheimer's, we may have increased the number of years of life, but not the quality. It will be an added expense for the family, the government, or both.

- Boomers were able to graduate from school and enter the job market with full-time jobs. Later generations often had to work a few years at less than desirable employment until they were able to get their career on track. Many had large student loans. These factors can restrict the ability of an individual to obtain service credits and save for retirement.

In the year 1900, there were approximately a dozen private pensions in the United States. Many men did not live past sixty-five and those who did survive were often still working. As a result, the first employers offering pensions only had to finance a short period between retirement and death. Since many workers died before they retired, the cost of pensions was not significant. One of the greatest changes over the past century is the length of retirement. A century ago, men were often forced to work until they were physically unable to perform their job. Retirement was often short since people worked longer and died sooner. The lack of a pension and minimal savings were a great motivation to keep working. Today it is common for individuals to retire before the age of sixty. Sometimes this is a choice made by the employee, other times the employer has taken the necessary steps to force a retirement before an individual is ready. It is not uncommon for a person to work for thirty-five years, retire and live for an additional thirty-five years. Thus, the employer received thirty-five years of service but provided salary and pensions that last seventy years. Defined benefit pension plans were one of the best gifts received by the boomers. Younger workers will have to save sufficient funds through their working years from investments and the use of tax-assisted retirement vehicles. Faced with the problems of finding well-paying jobs, raising a family and paying for their children's education, many families will struggle to fund their retirement.

Many retired couples may have parents to support that require some level of physical or financial support. At the same time, they may have children who have either never left home or returned after a failed marriage or a career that did not work out as expected. If a retired couple is financially independent, they may be able to afford the assistance of support workers to help care for their parents, but the demand on time and emotions can be exhausting. However, if they are struggling to pay their bills, while caring for parents and/or children at this phase of their life, it will not only be stressful but may reduce savings at a much faster rate than they anticipated when they planned their retirement.

Funding Retirement

When planning for retirement, it should be considered to have three distinct phases:

- go
- go slow
- no go

The "go" phase is the initial phase of retirement when individuals have their health and sufficient money to enjoy the pleasures life has to offer. This often involves spending on hobbies and travel. For many families, this is the greatest period of their lives.

The "go slow" segment commences when the health of one of the spouses starts to decline and activities are curtailed. By the age of seventy, many people have some body part that is not working properly and are seeing a specialist to manage the issue.

"No go" is the final stage when they can no longer live in their home and require additional support to perform the basic functions of life. Mobility is an issue and mental functions may be deteriorating.

Planning for retirement requires a calculation of how much money is required to fund each phase. The "go" and "go slow" phases are usually not problematic as the family can match their lifestyle to the available financial resources. The "no go" phase will be a significant issue for the next few decades as boomers move past healthy retirement into a period that requires assistance. Picture the boomers as a demographic spike that will reach a point when they can no longer care for themselves and this will create tremendous health care costs and a crisis to house these elderly people. The fortunate ones have families to provide care and accommodation, but many do not have this option.

In addition to the substantial number of people requiring assistance, medical science will continue to pump out medicines and treatments that will increase life expectancy. Increased longevity is desirable if individuals can maintain their health and do not run out of cash. Longer life spans for individuals with excellent pensions and a large investment portfolio may be desirable, but for those without pensions who have depleted their savings and are living off government pensions, longevity will not be without its issues.

Women and Retirement - Women tend to have a longer life expectancy than men and utilize a greater share of nursing home beds. Since they are the largest component of the "no go" segment of retirees, they are at the greatest risk of running out of money. Many retired females from the boomer generation did not work their entire career which impacts their potential pension income. If their spouse's pension were the primary source of retirement income, there would be a substantial reduction of income upon his death. Either the pension stops or is replaced by a significantly reduced survivor benefit. A longer life and reduced income mean that retirement may start off well, but the final years may be a challenge to fund while living in a dignified manner. This issue may be reduced in the future as women spend more time in the workforce and the realities of full-time jobs may start to even out the life span differential between men and women. As female boomers retire and require increased assistance in their final years, it will create a tremendous burden on governments. There will be increased health care costs, a lack of retirement homes and too many seniors fighting to stay above the poverty line. As deficits continue to increase, this will be another financial priority that strains government resources.

Health Care Limbo - When families reach a point they cannot look after a loved one, they are faced with the issue of finding suitable accommodation. The number of boomers in frail condition will soon start to overwhelm the available senior living accommodations and palliative care facilities. Families face a major crisis if they cannot provide care and there are no spaces available. Many families that are denied accommodation struggle on, but some use a tactic of last resort. They call an ambulance and have the family member sent to the emergency ward of the local hospital. Once the patient is assessed and possibly treated, the family advises they can no longer provide care and the health care system is forced to find accommodation. This often results in a placement in less than ideal conditions, but too many families believe they have no other option.

Bottom Line - Unless you are wealthy, a high-income earner or a member of generous defined benefit pension plan, it will be a struggle to enjoy a middle-class lifestyle during retirement. We may lack suitable accommodations and health care resources to care for our loved ones in their final years. This is a foreseeable crisis that will require the expenditure of vast sums of money. It does not appear governments are taking the necessary steps to get in front of the issue.

At a time when retired families require increased assistance, an overextended government may be forced to reduce the services they offer to seniors. Possible reductions in health care spending or other critical services will introduce more families to retirement hell.

CHAPTER TEN

POST-TRUTH SOCIETY

You will be judged on your last bad act,
not your good intentions

Is truth an ideal that has lost its value in a world that places a greater emphasis on victory than fair play and sportsmanship? In the days of the greatest generation truth was a virtue. People have always lied to get out of trouble or avoid responsibility, but there appears to be a fundamental change as being open, honest and transparent is no longer an expectation of our political leaders, institutions, or businesses. Perhaps the new normal is that when a politician speaks, it should be taken in context, but not literally. There have always been two distinct levels of lying. White lies are considered acceptable and are social niceties used to avoid hurting someone's feelings, as compared to dishonesty as a tactic to gain an advantage or avoid negative consequences. However, between the two extremes of absolute truth and outright lies are many shades of gray. There are half-truths, lies of omission, broken promises, exaggerations and compulsive lying by those with low self-esteem. Some lie because of circumstances, while others are sociopaths and lying is ingrained in their personality. It can also result from youth and immaturity. We do not expect a three-year-old always to tell the truth and we can often know that teenagers are lying because their mouth is moving.

When my daughter was a precocious eight-year-old she asked the following question - Dad, do you believe in the four magic men. Not having heard the expression "magic men," I asked who they were and she said they were Santa Claus, the Easter Bunny, the Tooth Fairy and God. I looked her in the eye and said, of course, I believe in them because they are real. I lied to my daughter and did not have the slightest regret. Is it wrong to lie to your children about Santa Claus? There is the classic question from a wife to her husband - "does this dress make me look fat." There is only one answer to that question even if she looks like Mama Cass on a bad day. A son visits his father who has dementia in a retirement home and he asks if he can move back home. Should the answer be direct and honest or should his feelings be taken into account? In polite society, we understand all brides look fantastic, all babies are beautiful, all children are above average and every boy has the world's best dog. In my case, the latter comment is true as we had the world's best dog and her name was Bailey. White lies provide an acceptable escape when being brutally honest would be hurtful and disrespectful. There is another type of lie that many consider being consistent with social conventions and that relates to answering intrusive questions. When people are questioned and the answer is either confidential or relates to information they are not prepared to share, civil conversation suggests that "it's none of your damn business" is not an appropriate response. Some people are naturally nosey while others have a private side and are not prepared to share certain information. The answer is not truthful, but it is just a polite way of not sharing the information. Politicians must be overwhelmed with such questions and it is understandable they do not want to give a full and truthful response to every question that is asked, especially since many questions have a hidden agenda.

We place a value on honesty and consider it to be a component of good character. However, is achieving the abstract principle of truth, more important that maximizing financial advantage, winning an election, selling a vehicle, seducing a woman, or avoiding the negative consequences of a thoughtless decision? If we were totally honest, it would be difficult to achieve many of our objectives, especially as there are minimal consequences for dishonesty. In most of these situations, there is no violation of the law and it is unclear if there is an expectation of truth from either party. When caught in some form of deception, it is often justified by the notion that is how business operates. A man can cheat his friends and keep that information from his wife who sees him as a loving and responsible spouse.

Moving beyond situations where an individual deceives another to gain some advantage, society appears to have lowered the bar on their expectations of truth from our various institutions. Perhaps we have entered a post-truth era where appeals are made to emotion, rather than relying on facts. Whether it is internet dating, resumes, politicians, or TV ads, who and what can we believe? If there are low expectations of truth telling, then trust will be one of the casualties. There was a time when reasonable people were entitled to their opinion, just not their own facts. With the internet and other dubious sources of information, our polarized society cannot agree on the facts.

One of the problems is how we receive our information. Gone are the days when we heard it on the news and therefore it was assumed to be true. We receive our information from various sources, but the traditional media is augmented by the internet and social media. People tend to get their information from a source that is consistent with their views. Opinion is mixed with facts and newscasts tend to let others express their views, rather than acting as an independent fact checker. Newscasts need ratings and controversies draw audiences. There was a day we knew something to be true because Walter Cronkite said so.

The public says they would like honesty from their elected representatives, but believe they are more are likely to hear talking points, spin, opinions, partial truths and responses that do not answer the question that was asked. Politicians tell tall tales such as:

- I became a politician to serve the people. Perhaps somewhere, once upon a time, a politician ran for elected office and the primary reason was to serve the public. It is a great line for canned speeches, but it's more often about fame, fortune, hubris, future opportunities and the exercise of power. If serving the public was their reason for getting into politics, it must be disappointing to discover the public thinks so little of their service. The gold standard for service to his country is Pat Tillman. He played football in the NFL for the Arizona Cardinals and when the season ended after terrorists attacked the twin towers; he walked away from a lucrative contract, joined the Army Rangers and went to Afghanistan to serve his country. In the most horrific of events, he was killed by friendly fire. How many politicians are hawks on foreign policy but took steps to ensure they never served in the military?
- When a politician has a new plan, the question arises as to how it will be paid for without raising taxes or increasing the deficit. The standard line is it will be paid by eliminating waste and corruption from the system. Whatever.
- The deficit will be reduced in the next fiscal year. The plan is simple as the economy will grow and

the government will receive more tax dollars and the deficit will be eliminated. Surprise, surprise, it's still there at the end of the next year.

- Vote for me and I will cut your taxes. Great rhetoric since the public wants lower taxes and it has been the mantra of politicians for many years. Given the number of elections in the last decade, have your taxes been reduced? Politicians might argue that although taxes have not been reduced, they increased at a lower rate than would have been possible if they had not been elected.

If a politician's objective was to cut spending and balance the budget, would announcing details of the spending reductions during the campaign help or hinder the possibility of being elected? One politician wisely noted that an election campaign was no place to have a frank discussion on policy.

When dealing with a sales rep, there is an expectation of some degree of puffery. This term is defined as a statement to promote a certain product and should be considered as subjective rather than objective. There is an assumption that no reasonable person would take the claim literally. A used car sales person might say the car was only driven on Sundays by a little old lady on her way to and from church. If after the purchase it was discovered she was an atheist and did not attend church, the sale still stands and no fraud was committed. Many sales reps exaggerate as the sale is more important than a truthful dissertation of the advantages and disadvantages of a product. If we consider politicians as sales reps and policy as their product, should we not expect some degree of puffery as part of their pitch? The public wants action to resolve our economic problems, but politicians often do not have the answers and it is not in their nature to admit such shortcomings.

As a culture, we have grown to accept avoiding the truth and deception as accepted strategies to achieve certain objectives. If there are no consequences for dishonest behavior and it helps achieve some objective, why be surprised if hearing the truth becomes less common? When dishonesty reaches the level of treachery, is that the time to draw a line in the sand?

Would there be any market for a daily newscast that only tells the truth? There would be no opinions, no stories that have not been fact checked, no discussion of both sides of an issue and no attempt to use controversy to boost ratings, just the news as it happened. It would not include any surrogates, no spinning of stories or debating the issues; just the truth. Imagine a newscast without any press releases from reality TV stars sharing their views on the events of the day. If we were extremely lucky, the announcers would not joke and giggle at each other's charming wit, while sportscasters would realize they are neither celebrities nor comedians. Inform us, don't try to entertain us.

We live in a world that is competitive and often mean-spirited. Many believe it is not possible to achieve success and always take the high road. It is not possible to play by the Marquess of Queensberry rules in a knife fight. Despite the lapse in truthfulness, honesty is still a trait that is admired by employers and people of character. Developing a moral compass will allow us to stand out in a world where truth is a tactic, rather than a requirement.

Bottom Line - Our worldview is an interpretation of reality. Everyone believes their perspective is fact based, but in a world where we cannot agree on the facts and the words of those who influence us may be biased, building trust and consensus are problematic. Back in the day, if President Kennedy or Eisenhower made a public statement, most of the society would accept the words at face value. If today's leaders make a statement they claim to be factual, is that a sufficient reason to believe them?

The enemy of misinformation is education combined with a certain degree of skepticism. As a young person, I took the word of authority figures as gospel. Whether it was my parents, a teacher or a political leader that made a statement, the truth was assumed. My first memory of challenging an official position was the investigation that followed the assassination of President Kennedy. My mindset was to believe media reports and government investigations, but in my thought process, the lone gunman theory was not the obvious conclusion of the facts. I was not convinced there was a conspiracy since there were unknowns, rather I did not believe the government was forthcoming. It appears one of the greatest strengths an individual can possess is knowing who to trust since the answer is no longer obvious.

CHAPTER ELEVEN

FANTASIES OF OUR GOVERNMENT AS SAVIOR

Stress is not having to sink a ten-foot putt to win the match; it is a single mother deciding between paying for rent or food

If the objective is to have a strong and growing middle class, it can only be accomplished with government leadership, but the polarization of politics, a focus on demonizing the opposition and a "gotcha" mentality has resulted in a large segment of the public losing faith in politicians. Governments do not create wealth, rather redistribute income and their success at generating opportunities for working families are poor. The public wants results, but that may be inconsistent with the politician's prime objective of staying in power.

Politicians conduct surveys to understand the issues that concern the electorate. It is usually some combination of economic growth, jobs, tax relief, immigration reform, government support programs or deficit control. Social justice tends not be a major plank in the campaign, rather a talking point used at partisan rallies. During election campaigns, they promise to resolve the issues of the day and argue the opposition parties are not prepared to make the tough decisions. In effect, they have become simplifiers. They take complex problems and promise

75

simple solutions. It is as if politicians have taken a parental role and try to explain the problems of the world to their children, the voters. Simple solutions are often false solutions, but it plays well to voter's concerns and fears. Traditional politicians tend to be incrementalists and their policy is often based upon small steady steps to resolve issues. A large segment of the electorate finds this too little, too late and wants action or at least the promise of a quick fix.

Have you ever met a federal politician? In all likelihood, they were impressive men and women and it was easy to have high expectations of what they will be able to accomplish. For the most part, they are phenomenal people, but the problem is normally not the people elected, but the political environment in which they operate. They may enter the world of politics with high ideals, but being subjected to party politics and the rigors of staying in office, it can change a person. Given access to power and so many people putting them on a pedestal, it is difficult for their heads not to grow and their initial idealism may give way to the realities of public life. If we throw out the bums in the next election and put in a new team, will anything change?

Public confidence in elected officials continues to fall, while parties and politicians outside the mainstream are gaining support around the world. This includes many potential leaders who have an autocratic nature and can create the belief that they are agents of change. There may be agreement on the need for change but there is a lack of consensus on what this entails, but it normally involves taking power away from the so-called elite and transferring it to the people. This type of power transfer can occur in revolutions, but not so frequently at the ballot box. There is a multitude of reasons for the negative view of politicians. However, it can often be traced back to a number of root causes:

- Politicians have a long history of over promising and under delivering.
- Despite their best intentions, there is often little they can do to resolve many of the problems we face without causing grief elsewhere in the economy.
- Potential solutions are approached from two perspectives. What is the best economic decision? Then it is viewed through their political lens to determine if the action will make their party look good or the opposition look bad. They understand that they can only achieve their objectives if they stay in power. Doing the right thing but losing votes is not seen as a wise course of action.
- They master rhetoric, spin and talking points, but the public has grown tired. There appears to be a game that politicians play and the public understands this dance and has tuned out.
- Almost everyone understands that our debt will restrain future generations, but most of the hard decisions to reduce it are politically unpopular and will cost votes. If the government cuts spending, the former recipients of those funds will be quite vocal and are quite effective at lobbying the government to maintain the status quo.
- The press has done a reasonable job of keeping voters informed and investigating ongoing scandals. However, some media sources have biases and tend to attract a like-minded audience. It can be troubling when news outlets combine opinion with fact and align their editorial comment with a particular political party or philosophy.

Perhaps there is a certain naiveté among the public that believes ideas are put forward during the campaign and an election ensures the best ideas win. It has been suggested that politics is like watching sausage get made. One may enjoy the final product, but the process may leave us uncomfortable.

Voters want jobs and economic growth, so politicians make it the cornerstone of their election campaign. Can you think of an election at any level - municipal, federal, state or provincial where the politicians have not said that jobs are their number one priority? Has anyone ever delivered on that promise in a meaningful way? Voters want jobs, lower taxes, safe streets and integrity from their elected officials. Politicians are gifted at identifying the needs of the voters and implying they have the power to fix the problems. Once in power, they often cannot deliver on their promises, since the economy may be impacted by global forces over which they have little control and the opposition can prevent or restrict proposed solutions. External forces include the price of oil, interest rates, currency fluctuations and the negative impact of globalization. When the next election rolls around, they repeat the promises, someone gets in power and the game is replayed. It is sort of like the watching the movie Ground Hog Day without the humor.

One of the lines that politicians love is "I have a plan for that." Regardless of the issue, it is easy to formulate a plan. Perhaps your seven-year-old son had a plan to be a major-league baseball player, or your daughter has a plan to be an Olympic swimmer. How did that workout? Anyone can have a plan for any complex issue such as health care, race relations or peace in the Middle East. Perhaps the question to ask these problem solvers is - give an example of a plan that has been successfully implemented on time and on budget. Most will be challenged to provide examples. There are so many plans, but very few effective implementations.

One of the more brilliant strategies made by all levels of government is to downplay issues related to debt. This is akin to boiling a frog in a pot of water, as the mountain of debt seems to be a distant problem for future generations to resolve. Perhaps government debt is the meanest trick boomers played on their children. They lived beyond their means and did it with the debt that will be repaid by the next generation. Politicians downplay the issue by keeping the focus on the deficit, rather than the debt. The deficit is the financial shortfall for the current year, while debt is the accumulated deficits from previous years.

Ronald Reagan suggested that government was the problem, rather than the solution. The expression "I am from the government and am here to help you" is a punchline of many comedians' jokes. How many young men and women graduated from college and said: "I want to be all that I can be and that is why I became a civil servant?"

Earlier we discussed the slow death of defined benefit pension plans in the private sector. The private sector understands the costs and risks associated with these plans, but this does not appear to be an issue for the public sector. Most civil servant pensions are the result of negotiations with unions representing government employees. When TV stations cover the negotiations, normally just before a strike deadline, take notice of the teams of negotiators for both sides. The government's team tend to wear expensive suits, possess business degrees, are well spoken and armed with data to support their position. The other side looks like a group of employees from any government office that could be residents of any middle-class neighborhood. Watching both groups enter the hotel to commence negotiations, it should be obvious this is not a fair fight. The union will win. The civil servants will keep their defined benefit pension plans and although management may try to get new employees to join a defined contribution plan, the union negotiators are normally able to nip this idea in the bud.

If the government has great negotiators and the facts to back up their position, why will the union prevail? They understand the public will not tolerate long strikes and as much as they complain about deficits, civil servant salaries or whatever, they want their services. The government of the day wants to be re-elected and it is better to settle disputes, even if there is a long-term cost to purchasing labor peace.

If we return to the three issues that resulted in boomer's apocalyptic legacy, do we believe our politicians can solve these problems that were previously laid out?

Debts and Deficits - Not likely. There is always hope the economy will grow and create more tax revenue, but cutting spending and cost control appears inconsistent with the goal of retaining power. They must eliminate the deficit in the current year and then run surpluses in future years that can be used to extinguish the accumulated debt. As for the issue of public service pension liabilities, unless there are some high-profile pension bankruptcies, progress on this issue will be very slow, if at all. Based upon recent history, the prognosis for success is low.

Boomer Spending in Retirement - There does not appear to be a political will to address this issue, so expect larger deficits. The taxes of the next generation will pay a significant portion of the boomer's final bill.

Environment and Climate Control - The public understands the problem, but there is a lack of consensus if we should pay the cost of addressing these issues because of the negative impact on the economy. We want more jobs and steps to be taken to control climate change and global warming, but these goals may be inconsistent. The good news is that more politicians on the conservative side of the political spectrum are starting to believe in a concept that most grade five kids understand. It's called science. Politicians will continue to make investments in new technologies related to the environment and claim victory. However, if we judge them based on quantitative measurements, success can be claimed when the trends are reversing, rather than "it would have been worse if we did nothing." There is an analogy of rearranging the deck chairs on the Titanic.

Most politicians want to resolve the issues facing the middle class, but there is a lack of consensus on the solutions. As long as the prime objective is to retain power at any cost, the most we can expect of the government are small positive steps in the right direction. Regardless of the ineffectiveness of our politicians, the government employs some incredible civil servants, central bankers and scientists who care about the middle class and are committed to doing the right thing. Whether or not it is politically expedient with the elected officials is a different issue. Perhaps governments can slow down the demise of the middle class; however, their ability to restore it to its former glory may be beyond their skill set.

Bottom Line – The path to the top for our elected officials is changing. It appears that having the best ideas is being replaced by name recognition and fame as a route to power. A personality cult, when combined with a focus on staying in power, may produce a victory but what is best for the political party may not be what is best for the country.

PART THREE

THE NEW FORMULA

The boomer's formula for success has been replaced by a more challenging path to a financially secure future. Competency, character, commitment and lifelong learning will be critical to an individual's ability to achieve his or her financial objectives.

CHAPTER TWELVE

PARADOX OF AN EDUCATION

It is genius to be the smartest person in the room and not let anyone know, but it easy to be the stupidest person and let everyone know

Individuals that graduated from university in 1970 had a straightforward path to financial security and a comfortable retirement. Circumstances have changed and a university degree no longer provides any guarantees. Too many recent graduates juggle part-time jobs and if they are lucky enough to find employment with a large organization, it is often contract work. Sometimes these short-term jobs lead to full-time employment, but often it does not. Many graduates have jobs that do not require a degree and their peers in the workplace are often high school graduates. This is especially true of liberal arts graduates, even though universities continue to suggest their students will acquire essential skills such as critical thinking and reflective reading.

We can debate the value of a university degree, but studies indicate there is a direct correlation between the level of education attained and an individual's income. University graduates earn more than those without a degree and a student who has not obtained a high school degree is worse off yet. Thus, we have the paradox of a university education. Those with a degree make more money on average than those that have not completed university. However, many who pursue the sheepskin may regret the decision if they cannot translate the degree into a career. The issue is determining the value proposition of an education. If the degree is financed by debt but provides no skills that employers value, the question has to be asked as to whether or not the degree is worth the cost?

We cannot blame the universities for doing their best used car sales pitch; given the profit margins on these courses. Acquiring a degree of dubious value may be time well wasted if parents paid for the schooling or the student won a scholarship which would allow graduation with a minimal level of debt. Students have an opportunity to take advantage of the non-academic side of university and it's a great place to grow up, sow a few wild oats and explore interests that were not available in high school. However, students may not have done themselves any favors if they graduate with a degree that does not include acquiring skills that employers find desirable. This problem is magnified if the student has incurred a large student loan and has insufficient income upon graduation to repay the debt in a reasonable time frame. Even worse are those cases when a student drops out after a couple of years of school with a large loan and no degree. In other cases, graduates may realize the major they selected has not led to a satisfactory job, so they return to school for a degree in a different field of study. Unfortunately, many of these students are carrying loans from their first degree.

It is dangerous to make blanket statements on the value of a university degree since they are not equal in preparation for entry into the job market. Professional degrees such as engineering, nursing, law, business, science and medicine continue to provide paths to a successful career, but there are more bumps in the road as these graduates compete with highly-skilled peers chasing fewer top-end jobs. Graduating with a prestigious degree from a top-shelf university can be extremely beneficial, but it can be difficult to achieve as the competition is very bright and the entrance requirements are high.

One of the options open to students after completing their degree is entrepreneurship. Many great companies, especially in the area of technology, were started in basements, garages and college dorms. However, many startups require capital and if the money has to be borrowed, a large student loan can make credit difficult to obtain. Students may graduate with the skill to start a potentially great company but cannot get financing because they incurred a large loan to pay for school. This supports the old saying that bank parking lots are the place that many new business ideas go to die.

Never buy the argument that obtaining a degree is the highest priority regardless of the major or the institution attended. When considering a specialization, it is clear that some are more valuable than others. For example, science and engineering will create better career path opportunities than degrees in the history of medieval Europe or women's studies. There are various tiers of universities and some of the lower-tier schools are diploma mills that have a questionable value in the job market. Graduate from Harvard, MIT, Caltech, Stanford, or any number of phenomenal schools, the world knows that something of value has been obtained. The simple fact that these elite schools have accepted the student is an indication of a gifted mind. However, an executive MBA from Timbuctoo Bible College that was taken over the internet and financed by a large student loan may not be taken seriously by companies looking for new employees. I am not sure if Starbucks would place value on that degree, as they tend to hire graduates with critical thinking and reflective reading skills that are taught in liberal arts courses.

Bottom Line - Graduating from university is no longer a guaranteed gateway to success. The goal is to attain a skill or competency from the best school or program possible. Whether an engineer or a plumber, obtain a skill and then excel at the chosen profession. To show up at an employer's door with a diploma in hand and the promise to try your best if given an opportunity requires an intense level of optimism or perhaps it is just a reflection of an individual's naiveté.

CHAPTER THIRTEEN

A NEW FORMULA

*One does not become wise by hearing
wise men say wise things*

Back in the day, when admission standards were not as strict, a person of average intelligence could graduate university and land a job with a major employer. In today's world, a graduate with intelligence is nothing special and intellect can be considered a commodity. An honors degree does not guarantee success in the workplace. Millions of people are intelligent, but if that is the sum of a person's skill set, what do they have to set them apart from the herd? Employers receive piles of resumes from people who are smart but have no other measurable skill. Even back in his day, President Calvin Coolidge believed education was not enough. He thought nothing was more common than unsuccessful men with great talent as education alone will not produce success since the world is full of educated derelicts.

Boomers that acquired a university degree had a high probability of successful careers, but current graduates, especially those with a liberal arts degree, may have student loans and a job rather than a career. If the formula for success in the boomer's day is outdated, how do individuals increase their chances of success in the economy of tomorrow? The new formula is based on the core principles of competency and character. Competency means not only possessing a valuable skill but being able to perform it with some level of excellence. Character is about values and doing the right thing and when combined with leadership skills, it is a trait valued by employers. A skill can be acquired, but character is more ambiguous as those lacking integrity may still claim it as part of their makeup. In addition to these traits, employers are looking for commitment and an appropriate attitude in new hires. These are difficult to measure, especially if the employee believes the commitment is a one-way street.

Competency

What is the most valuable asset of individuals entering the workforce? It is not a house or car, but a skill that can be sold to earn income. If the skill is lifting heavy things or flipping small things like hamburgers, the pay is modest, advancement opportunities are limited and job security is tenuous. However, if the skill is designing computer applications or unclogging pipes, not only will the pay be higher, but multiple paths are available to a financially secure future.

An executive from a large technology company was quoted as saying that a top engineer is at least 300 times more valuable than one with average skills. There is an important difference between being among the top ten percent in a given field and convincing others that it is the appropriate ranking. Graduating from a top school with high marks sends a message to the world. Graduates from elite universities may have a greater opportunity to excel as large employers often have a fast track program for these recruits.

In 1960, a high school degree was a sufficient education for most jobs. In 1980, a university degree would lead to a reasonable paying job. Currently, a degree suggests the individual is of at least of average intelligence, but so are thousands of other graduates looking for work. The objective is no longer just to have a degree but also have a skill or competency. If the skill is complimented by a degree, this is a superior option and if it is from a prestigious university, better still.

It is sad when students complete a university degree but do not possess any skills valued by employers, other than as a unit of labor that can be trained to perform a task in a few hours. Our education system does not prioritize ensuring that every graduate possesses some expertise. However, selecting a skill to pursue is not just a decision for students leaving high school. Regardless of where people are on their career path, everyone should focus on ensuring they excel at something. For those that do not possess a skill, it is important to be proactive and acquire one. If the only skill is a perceived ability to manage and supervise people, it would be foolish to think other employers will recognize and embrace these proficiencies. I have little doubt that every bad boss I ever had thought they were great managers and leaders of people. The path to acquiring a skill can start at any age; however, there are more obstacles once individuals reach their mid-twenties. This may include both financial and family obligations, plus the belief they are too old to change course.

Depending upon which skills an individual possess, the compensation can vary significantly. Let's consider the case of two brothers, Bart and Frank. Bart attended a community college and apprenticed to become a plumber. Frank attended medical school and is a successful family physician. Is it obvious which brother earned the higher salary last year? The most apparent answer would be Frank since family doctors earn excellent compensation and his practice is thriving. Plumbers may not have ideal working conditions, but they possess skills that translate into a comfortable middle-class lifestyle. A few years after getting his papers, Bart started his own plumbing business and then opened shops in six nearby communities. He has seventy-five employees and the business continues to expand. Would it be surprising if Bart made twice as much as his brother?

If an individual has a skill, such as carpentry, brain surgery, computer programming or preparing corporate tax returns, these skills are more valuable than stocking shelves or working at a takeout window. Possessing a skill that employers value may result in greater employment opportunities and may present entrepreneurial options.

Regardless of the skill, individuals want to be considered above average in their area of competency. There is a marketing component to convince others of the high level of expertise that is possessed. The status of the school or institution that provided the skill is important. Two law school graduates could apply for a job. One has a degree from the Law School at Timbuctoo Bible College and the other graduated in the top 10% of his class from Harvard Law School. One can never be certain which will eventually become the better lawyer, but 99.9999% of the time it is the Harvard graduate. The Timbuctoo Bible College does present one clear advantage over the competition as their graduates will be significantly cheaper to hire.

By the time students are seniors in high school, they should identify the skills they wish to acquire and the steps necessary to make it happen. The final step is to determine the market for that skill upon graduation. Consider the following examples:

- A large university had an excellent program for training teachers. However, for various reasons, school boards were not hiring. It was probable that not one graduate would receive a full-time teaching job upon graduation. They still had options such as supply teaching that may lead to a full-time job or teaching English overseas.

Despite the oversupply of teachers, the University kept turning out more graduates and new students continued to enroll.

- After completion of a law degree, graduates have to complete an articling term before they can practice law. The articling process is also an audition for full-time employment if the partners are satisfied with student's work and professionalism. However, many of the gold star firms have cut back on the number of articling students they hire, creating more competition for the top spots while others are challenged to find a position.

- Many professions have subtle methods of controlling the number of members that can apply their trade. Individuals must determine if they can move to another jurisdiction and apply their craft without some recertification or waiting period.

Technology is changing jobs and industries. Education and training cannot stop once a student has entered the workforce. Many employers are committed to upgrading their employee's skills and are willing to pay the training costs. Investing in training and certifications should provide an ongoing payback throughout a career. It may lead to a new job or retaining their current job when co-workers are being let go. However, not all courses are of equal value. Courses on leadership, team building, the value of diversity and the employer's latest management fad may be time well spent, or not. During my time in the corporate world, one of our latest management fads was Six Sigma and the training was a week of my life that I shall never get back. It must have been important since the corporate speak crowd who think outside the box and find synergy in every project, was sure it was going to become part of our corporate DNA. However, the focus must be on staying on the leading edge of knowledge in your field of expertise and continuing to stay current on job-related technologies.

Educational Timing - It's time to throw our model of educational timing out the window and replace it with the philosophy of life-long learning. Perhaps it takes three to four years to acquire a competency, but too many people assume that the time frame must be immediately after high school. This may be the ideal time, but if a career is not unfolding as expected, a person must be prepared to go back to school whether they are thirty, forty or fifty. Some high school graduates pursued the wrong skill, whereas others are not that good at the skill they selected. It's great to be an electrician unless the individual is the worst electrician in the city.

Education in western cultures is based on the theory of getting a fundamental education in public and high school and then the student has the option of pursuing a higher education that may or may not result in the acquisition of a skill. Whether it is a law degree or a plumbing apprenticeship, these skills are normally acquired when individuals are aged eighteen to twenty-three. Some may return to school if their careers did not work out as expected, but this option is seldom exercised. One major exception is returning to pursue an MBA. This can be a difficult value proposition calculation as the courses are expensive, salary has been forfeited by returning to school and the job market and future salary are never guaranteed upon graduation. There are elite schools that offer such programs and there are also colleges like the Timbuctoo Bible College, which has an MBA program that has low entrance requirements, courses can be taken over the internet and financing options are available. As for job prospects, you may want to ask your server at the local pub, as he may be a graduate.

A plant closes and workers are forced to the unemployment lines. They could select lower paying service jobs or the disability option, but a better choice is returning to school. It would make little sense to go university and get a degree in European history, but an apprenticeship in one of the trades may hold promise. Men who were downsized in the manufacturing sector may have a mechanical aptitude that translates very well into the various skilled trades. If manufacturing companies have fewer employees in the future, there may be opportunities in construction. This newly acquired skill can also provide a path to entrepreneurship.

When workers are downsized, they may struggle to pay for an education but financial assistance is available for most courses after high school and debt must be considered an investment in one's future. Once a skill has been acquired, the individual must be prepared to move where the jobs are located. Going back to school and relocating after graduation is a challenge for many families, but it beats the alternatives.

Character

Employers want to hire individuals with a high level of character, which may consist of work ethic, honesty, doing the right thing, taking responsibility, etc. However, even though employers want character, most potential employees claim to be honest and this includes the lazy, the dishonest, criminals, sociopaths and scoundrels. This is further complicated as ethics are situational. Integrity can be more challenging when no one is watching and there is no chance of being caught when acting inappropriately. Under once set of circumstances, people may be stand-up individuals and do the right thing, whereas, in other situations, they may not. In many organizations, it is difficult to get rid of a problem employee, so if the character deficiency is not identified in the hiring process, it may fester for years.

Strong character is normally the foundation of great leaders, but it is important to distinguish between leaders and managers. Leadership has a positive connotation, whereas the term boss is neutral as they can be good, bad or horrible. Just because someone is the boss, does not imply the possession of any leadership skills. The standard definition of a leader is a person who has been given authority to lead. However, there is a higher standard of leadership and people with this attribute can inspire, motivate and achieve goals that may be unattainable with someone else in charge. Too often being a leader is simply finding a parade and getting in front of it.

A trench warfare example outlines differences in leadership styles. The location is France in the year 1917 and soldiers are living in trenches a few hundred yards from the enemy. Orders had been received from a general in a far-off location that at noon the troops will attack the enemy. There is an understanding there will be significant casualties on both sides. The officer in charge has three options to get his troops to advance towards enemy gunfire:

- Order the troops to attack because it is an order from headquarters.
- Tell the troops to charge, or they will be shot.
- Lead the soldiers into harm's way.

Which style of leadership is more effective regarding the soldier's morale and confidence? The leaders that chose the third option have a greater probability of future promotion, assuming they survive the attack.

Many years ago, I had a boss who met my gold standard of leadership. This was during a period when the company was stressing the importance of leadership and they hired an endless procession of business professors to teach this noble art. This included the standard leadership attributes of having a vision, living corporate values, aligning corporate goals to personal goals, etc. One of the tasks was to rate our bosses on these attributes so they could develop an action plan to become better leaders. My boss did not receive high ratings on the various leadership attributes, as it was not his style to sit around and share his vision and perform all the other activities great leaders do on a daily, if not hourly basis. Despite the poor rankings, he was considered by his direct reports to be a great leader, mentor and an executive without equal within the company. This raises the question, how could an individual that did not rank very high on the standard leadership scales be such an inspirational leader? His attributes can be summarized as:

- A gentleman in the classic sense who showed respect towards everyone in every interaction.
- When he gave his word, it was considered gospel.
- He was never political and led his subordinates, rather than attempting to "manage up" to impress his superiors. He cared about his staff and he had their back.

There is a depressing aspect of this story. His staff considered him a great leader because he was honest, respectful, non-political and would never advance his career on the backs of his employees. These have become increasingly rare characteristics in a world where many bosses would throw employees under the bus to advance their career. Good character is the foundation of a great boss.

Bottom Line - Competency, character, commitment and lifelong learning are the keys to a successful career. It is also the skill set of many leaders and our world could use a few more great leaders.

CHAPTER FOURTEEN

FINANCIAL STRATEGIES

All of us are smarter than any one of us

The financial planning strategies utilized by boomers will continue to be important and this includes tax planning, investment strategies, insurance coverage and retirement planning. For the financially secure, the future may be a continuation of current practices. However, for many families the world has not unfolded as expected and the future is frightening. Some of the more disconcerting trends include:

- Many families are carrying a high debt load that may have accumulated from student loans, periods of unemployment, large mortgages or income levels that are too low to build an emergency fund. Increased debt can result in a lower level of savings in an era where funding retirement is a lifelong process.
- The concept of cradle to grave employment is becoming increasingly rare. This has implications for years of pensionable service, seniority and possible periods of unemployment.
- The drastic decline in defined benefit pensions plans has made funding a retirement more

challenging. If interest rates remain low and employees make their investment decisions, the level of retirement income may be significantly less than amounts enjoyed by previous generations.

- Inadequate pension income may impact the projected dates of retirement. Many individuals may have to work past their targeted date to maintain their financial independence. Conversely, many workers will be forced from their jobs before they are financially prepared to retire and it will be a challenge to find high-paying jobs at this age.

- The introduction of disruptive technologies will result in the elimination of jobs, companies and entire industries. Movement of employees within an industry has been common, but this option may no longer be available if entire industries disappear. Consolidations within an industry will result in fewer employment opportunities.

- The nature of work will continue to change to the detriment of employees. As governments continue to increase payroll taxes, companies will respond in various ways, none of which are favorable for workers. Moving jobs offshore will continue to be an option if profits are squeezed. Employers may prefer contract staff and part-time workers to full-time employees.

Financial Strategies for a More Challenging Future

Many families will continue to prosper, but saving for retirement while paying for a house and their children's education may be problematic. As a result, families should consider some financial strategies that have been around for years but have taken a backseat to more conventional planning. These include:

- Using your home to fund retirement
- Global mobility
- Prepayment of inheritances
- Rethinking the 4% solution
- Building a long-term investment plan

Using a Home to Fund Retirement – When boomers found their first jobs, they were often attracted by the starting salary, rather than possible retirement benefits, as many twenty-three-year-olds did not place much value on a pension plan. Flash forward to the boomer's retirement phase and many are receiving payments from defined benefit pensions, plus income from investments and government pensions. Taking a job over thirty years ago with a generous defined benefit pension may have been more lucky than smart, but we are allowed to feel good about decisions made early in life that turned out well.

If workers project their potential retirement income, they may be in for a shock. To meet their retirement objectives, they need significant savings and higher rates of return that can be achieved on fixed-income investments. How does one achieve such a high rate? One possible solution is speaking with a mutual fund sales rep, who prefers the title financial planner and select various higher risk funds that are capable of providing the necessary returns. The sales rep can provide a listing of funds whose past performance has been excellent and the implication is that such returns will continue, but as the fine print says - past returns are no guarantee of future performance. Even if there was a great return on the various emerging market or small cap funds in the past few years, they could reverse direction and generate significant losses. Risk and volatility are dangerous paths to financial security. It may be too easy to chase rates of return and ignore the associated risks, but such options may look attractive if interest rates stay low.

One solution is to save until it hurts and cut back on lifestyle expenditures to generate more capital to invest. However, many young couples are not prepared to sacrifice lifestyle for a retirement that is decades away as they are optimistic about their future. Paying for a dream home while setting aside funds for retirement will be a challenge for many families. Many boomers with defined benefit pensions could save for a house and retirement would take care of itself. If a family can eliminate their mortgage, the equity in the home presents some options. If the home is located in a large city with an expensive housing market, the family can sell the house and move to a smaller community with more reasonable prices. It is not easy to move away from friends and family at retirement, but this tactic can generate positive cash flow. A lesser advantage can be attained by downsizing within the same city. This may be more beneficial for individuals in the final phase of retirement when mobility is an issue.

Another option is obtaining a reverse mortgage on the property. To understand the workings of this product, let's assume is home is worth $400,000 and based on the age of the owners and location of the property, the family will qualify for a $250,000 reverse mortgage. There are options how the family can receive the money, but let's assume they take a lump-sum payment. The family has $250,000 in the bank and a mortgage of an equal amount on their home. The beauty of this product is the loan does not have to be repaid until the home is sold, the spouses move, or they are both deceased. If we assume the value of the reverse mortgage was $350,000 and the home was worth $500,000 when the last spouse dies, the beneficiary receiving the home has some options. The house can be sold and the proceeds of the sale can extinguish the debt and the beneficiaries retain the balance. It is also possible for the beneficiaries to retain the home by refinancing the $350,000 loan.

A loan that never has to be repaid may sound like an ideal solution, but there is a downside and it is a major issue. The family has utilized the equity in the home to fund retirement, rather than leaving it for their beneficiaries. Returning to our example, if the family had one child who will inherit the entire estate, if there were no reverse mortgage the child would inherit an asset worth $500,000. However, once the reverse mortgage is eliminated, the equity in the home is reduced to $150,000. A reverse mortgage may be an ideal product for a couple with no children as funding retirement can take precedence over the needs of beneficiaries. Parents must decide if they want to use the equity in their home to fund their retirement or leave it to their children as part of the estate. It's a tough call for many families.

There are some concerns with reverse mortgages, such as fees and the rate of interest charged on the loan, but it may be an ideal option for some families. In the United States, there have been some unscrupulous players in this market, so it would be wise to have a lawyer review any contract before being signed. It is important to have both spouses named on the deed. One area of concern is the date the last spouse leaves the home and thereby triggers the repayment clause. There have been issues when the last surviving spouse moves to a nursing home and therefore the debt must be repaid, even though the owners assumed the debt would be repaid after death. If there is someone else living in the home when the last spouse dies, that individual may have to vacate the property.

When considering a reverse mortgage one of the key considerations is the rate of interest on the loan. Typically, a home equity loan will have a lower rate of interest than a reverse mortgage. Consideration may be given to taking out a home equity loan, but the issue is how and when the amount will be paid back. The reverse mortgage is paid back after death, so it is not the homeowner's issue. The choice between the types of debt will have a significant impact on the beneficiaries of an estate.

Mobility - Whether it was the Irish leaving for North America because of the potato famine or the poor from neighboring countries hoping for a better life, immigration has always been part of our society. One of the latest trends in immigration is the number of refugees who want to escape war and terror in their homeland. The main reason for immigration has always been to find greater opportunities, but it is raising concerns for both governments and workers who feel their position in society is being challenged. There are issues such as the assimilation into the community and how to handle those that do not follow the rules of their new host country.

Historically, lower-skilled individuals relocated to parts of the country that were hiring. When the industrial revolution started, young men moved from the farm to the city in search of employment. In recent years, families moved west for greater opportunities. In the future, mobility will undergo another change as more moves will be international and those moving will be highly-skilled workers moving to countries where their talents are valued. Some governments are attempting to keep out low-skilled workers, but ease the transition of those with needed proficiencies. It is becoming common for governments to set up systems to allow only the most qualified immigrants to become residents. Workers whose skill has become obsolete or undervalued in their current locale should consider global opportunities. It does not have to be forever, but seeking out international opportunities can be a phenomenal opportunity for a family to see the world. This option can be complicated if the spouse has a secure job or the family has a fifteen-year-old daughter. Good luck with one.

Pre-Payment of Inheritances – In a typical estate plan, upon the death of one spouse, the surviving spouse inherits the assets. Upon the death of the second spouse, the assets are distributed to the beneficiaries, normally the children and grandchildren. However, as seniors are often living into their late eighties and early nineties, it is not unusual for beneficiaries to receive their inheritance after they retire. However, from a need perspective, the beneficiaries could have used these funds twenty years earlier when they were struggling with mortgage payments and paying for their children's education.

If a family has more resources than required to fund retirement, consideration may be given to distributing assets before their death. The prepayment of an inheritance can be a godsend for children that are struggling. The amount of any prepayment can be a difficult decision, especially in cases of second marriages and stepchildren. As parents age, they may become more conservative and if they are experiencing a level of mental slowdown, they may be unwilling to face an issue that will solve itself once they die. Once a retired couple calculates the amount of capital required to fund their retirement, consideration should be given to the prepayment of inheritances.

Rethinking the 4% Solution- It was an idea developed by Bill Bengen who graduated from The Massachusetts Institute of Technology. It was an excellent rule of thumb to ensure one did not run out of funds during retirement. It assumed a balanced portfolio and the strategy was to withdraw 4% of the family's nest egg every year during retirement. In each subsequent year, the 4% would be increased by the rate of inflation to maintain purchasing power. It was a useful guide to determine the rate at which investments should be liquidated. For example, if a family had $1,000,000 in the savings, they should withdraw $40,000 per year.

This rule of thumb should be downgraded to a rough guideline, as there have been some changes since the formula was devised. We have been in an extended period of low interest rates, plus life expectancies are increasing. It assumes linear withdrawals, but a family's cash flow needs can vary from year to year. Corrections to the stock market and their timing can impact the size of the nest egg. Do not accept the 4% rule as gospel. However, it can provide insight.

Another way to use the 4% rule is to determine the amount of capital required to fund retirement. Multiply the annual investment income required times twenty-five and this is the size of the target portfolio. If a family's objective is $100,000 per year, they should target a portfolio of $2,500,000 and utilize the 4% rule. This raises an obvious follow-up question as to how the family is going to save this amount.

Building a Long-Term Investment Plan - In the past, financial planners suggest building a personal safety net of at least six month's salary. This is still sound advice, but the focus has to change from a short-term safety net to a life-long strategy to fund retirement. Lacking wealth, high income, or a generous pension plan, retirement will not take care of itself, unless living off government assistance is an acceptable option. Given future uncertainties, a long-term investment plan must be a prime financial planning objective and this normally requires a cutback in consumption. The middle class is not a private club, but being a member can eliminate many of the financial burdens that restrict us from fulfilling our aspirations.

In addition to funding retirement, a long-term investment plan can be invaluable to fund periods of unemployment. The philosophy of living for today and letting tomorrow take care of itself is not a strategy that will work for most families. This is a classic trade-off of short-term consumption to enjoy the moment vs. a long-term plan to fund retirement. Playing the long game and prioritizing future goals is inconsistent with the action of too many families.

Bottom Line – Funding retirement will be a major issue for many families that work in the private sector. It will mean saving until it hurts, purchasing a smaller house than the contemplated dream home and focusing on the rate of return on investments. It is difficult to convince young people under the age of thirty that funding retirement is a critical priority, but it is a necessity that can be planned for or a regret that can be expressed in later years. As they hit retirement and lack the necessary investments, it is not helpful to fall back on the lament of people who made bad decisions – would have, could have, should have, won't help me now. As a wise man once said – you should have saved when you were younger. Cutting back on consumption and saving until it hurts may not sound like an ideal solution, but for many, it is the only way to have a dignified retirement.

PART FOUR

WORLDVIEW

Worldview is a term that encompasses our attitudes, beliefs and interpretation of reality. In the final chapters, I shall share a perspective on issues such as financial planning, happiness and obtaining advice, while maintaining a skeptical view of those who claim to be acting in our best interests.

CHAPTER FIFTEEN

Does Money Buy Happiness?

Stimulating people talk about ideas, while the less interesting talk about other people

Although most people work to support their lifestyle, certain individuals are motivated by non-financial considerations. This includes missionaries, employees at various charities, or those who follow their dreams regardless of the compensation. Perhaps the goal is to play in a band, become an actor, spend their days painting, or writing poetry. These pursuits could lead to a major payday, but in most cases, it is about the love of the craft. Too often these dreams die when the reality of family and responsibility takes over and the passion reverts to a hobby. Many people never follow their dream and wonder what would have happened if they followed their heart, rather than chase the almighty dollar. Money can buy almost anything, but let's explore whether or not it can buy happiness.

Money can be used for four purposes:

1. Pay taxes to the various levels of government which is a consequence of earning income.
2. The purchase of goods and services.

3. It can also be used as a legacy that can be passed on to our beneficiaries, normally children and grandchildren.
4. Spent to make the world a better place. This can include donations and gifts to support various causes.

We can assume the first option does not result in happiness, but the final three options can be great sources of pleasure. Many are focused exclusively on consumption as either there is insufficient family income or disinterest in the other options.

What do we mean by the term happiness? If a person wins a $1,000 in a lottery, it will cause an increase in the level of happiness for a few hours or days, but it has no impact over the next few decades. The term happiness relates to that general sense of contentment that we experience in life. The three sources of happiness are genetics, personal circumstances and life choices. Research indicates that genetics is the most important component of happiness. Certain people go through life with a perpetual smile on their face, while others exude negativity and suck the air out of any room they enter. Optimistic individuals tend to have a higher level of happiness than those with a more pessimistic outlook. Personal circumstances include financial issues, the state of a person's health and the well-being of family members. The third component of happiness relates to life choices that we make and includes social engagement, hobbies, passions and spending time with loved ones.

Money will not impact one's genetic makeup, but it can impact circumstances and life choices. Studies suggest that individuals making over $75,000 are more satisfied than those under this threshold. The $75,000 threshold is not a magic line, as it could just as easily be $62,000 or $77,000 and can vary by geography. Families that struggle to pay the bills and keep a roof over their head will be subject to more stress as they are constantly facing issues of insufficient money and there are no additional funds to make pleasurable choices such as travel or hobbies. It is a challenge to be truly happy and live in poverty.

There are other factors that impact levels of happiness, such as the aspirations of the individual. If individuals have unrealistic expectations of their place in the world, it can lead to grief. Jealousy is not a trait consistent with happiness. High-income earners fall on both sides of the debate. Some people define themselves by their vocation and a high salary brings a personal sense of satisfaction. However, some financially successful people believe their job has too much stress and takes time away from family and hobbies.

Money aside, one great source of happiness is a marriage where both partners love and respect each other. A cause of unhappiness is a bad marriage where the spouses have gone beyond being in love and have developed a level of dislike for their partner

Bottom Line - Happiness is primarily the result of one's genetic makeup, personal circumstances and life choices. However, having sufficient income to provide a reasonable living for one's family can reduce many of the day-to-day stresses that create a level of unhappiness. Money can buy happiness to a point, but once that threshold is reached, there is a minimal correlation between levels of income and happiness.

CHAPTER SIXTEEN

SEXUAL CURRENCY

Cute fades, but dumb is forever

Picture a couple walking down the street holding hands. She is in her early thirties, well dressed and drop dead gorgeous. The gentleman is in his late fifties, has a bit of a paunch, somewhat shorter than his lady friend and would never be mistaken for George Clooney. We know nothing about the couple, their background or the circumstances that led to their current relationship. Many people would draw the simple conclusion that he has money. Perhaps it is sexist or maybe just unfair that people who are more attractive have opportunities that are not available to others. There are purists who believe that physical attributes should not be relevant, as it is sexist and just wrong. Consider the following situation from the perspective of a young lady holding such views. A friend who is a Hollywood agent can set her up on a date with her choice of two men to an upcoming movie premiere. The choices are Brad Pitt or the star of a TV show called "Men who Weigh 500 Pounds." As a non-sexist female, it would not be possible to make a decision until more information is ascertained concerning the personality and character of both gentlemen. We can be certain that our idealistic and principled young lady will ask some relevant questions and after a period of quiet contemplation, she would select Mr. Pitt.

During the boomer's high school years, attractive women were seldom interested in the nerds and geeks who played chess, wore thick glasses and never played for a high school sports team. This was often a reasonable choice for many of these young men may have lacked the physical strength for blue-collar work and had no obvious career path in the 50s and 60s. However, some young men went to university and were attracted to new courses in the field of computer technology and this included Bill Gates, Paul Allen, Steve Jobs and Eric Schmidt. I am not sure if they qualified as nerds in their youth, but they may not have been the first choice of the hiring manager at the local factory had they applied for a position once they graduated high school. One great example of young men seeking the ideal women was the case of Jerry Hall. She was a beautiful model and mothered four children with Mick Jagger of the Rolling Stones. Once they split up in 1999, she was reported to have dated Paul Allen of Microsoft fame. Allen was also rumored to have dated tennis player Monica Seles. I have no knowledge of Paul Allen as a young man, but I cannot image him sitting in his bedroom listening to the Rolling Stones and believing that someday he would date Mike Jagger's old girlfriend. Dating super models and star athletes were only a teenage boy's wildest fantasy.

It is a fact of life that attractive women can open doors with just a smile. Sexual currency is defined as how a person uses their sexuality to gain some opportunity or advantage. It can include physical appearance, charisma, confidence, flirtation and charm, but rarely includes sexual relations. Most people understand how to increase their attractiveness or desirability to the opposite sex or same sex depending on the circumstances. Looking one's best, whether for a job interview, a night on the town or a trip to the grocery store is human nature for many people, perhaps not so much for a few Walmart shoppers. How people spend their sexual currency to attain advantages is a personal choice that may backfire or have unintended consequences. Too many teenagers have spent their currency to obtain drugs or date the handsome rebel. Although it may have made sense at the time, in hindsight they understand the cost of misspending their currency at a young age.

Discrimination is wrong and that includes looks, height and weight. Physical appearance should have no impact on an individual's ability to do her job. Visit a pub for a beer after work and odds are the hostess and server are attractive. This is no longer a female issue since most male servers have some combination of looks and charisma. An overweight, unattractive server could be phenomenal at her job, but she may never be hired to show her skills.

Studies have shown that tall people have higher incomes than shorter people. The CEOs of large corporations tend to be taller than average. Obese applicants often claim they were not hired due to their appearance, but it is difficult to prove. If two females apply for a job and they are otherwise equal in their skills, will the male manager let physical attractiveness be the deciding factor? If attractiveness was the determining factor, there is no doubt the individual responsible for hiring would settle on some other job-related skill as the basis for the hiring decision.

If people make themselves more attractive, through exercise, surgery or fashionable attire, should that be considered an investment in their future earning power or ability to attract a high-income spouse? We shall not dwell on mate selection or hooking up opportunities; rather the focus will be on the impact of sexual currency on an individual's financial well-being.

One of the misconceptions concerning sexual currency is that it includes having sex with someone to gain an advantage. That may happen, but it is the exception, rather than the rule. Let's assume a HR manager is interviewing three candidates for a position and all are equally qualified. Although the paperwork may suggest that one candidate is slightly more qualified than the others, the human resources manager may hire the cutest candidate for no other reason than she was the most physically attractive. It was her attractiveness that was the deciding factor and in no way was she flirtatious or acted less than professional. The HR manager who made the hiring decision made no sexual advances or inappropriate suggestions towards the new hire. Over the course of her employment, the relationship between the HR manager and the new employee was always professional. There was no sex, no suggestion of sex, or any relationship outside of work, but sexual currency was involved in the hiring decision. The young lady had sexual capital, but having it does not mean it has to be spent. There are companies that want to present a certain image to the world and may hire good looking and outgoing staff to validate their strategy.

There is a large company whose culture was to rarely fire employees for poor performance. The manager in charge of the department that recruited many university graduates into the company had a theory of hiring women. When interviewing candidates, he found that many applicants appeared to be suitable for the position and from this pool he would hire based on appearance, if all other factors were considered equivalent. He was happily married and had no interest in a non-professional relationship with any female that was hired into his department. His practice was based on the theory that if the young lady's performance were not up to standards and corporate policy would not permit him to fire the employee; it was easier to transfer an attractive female, than one who did not present herself well. Some young ladies were hired because of their sexual currency, but they had no reason to believe it was a factor in the hiring decision.

Let's examine some areas where relationships can have a significant impact on a person's financial position. Marriage is an economic partnership. Most couples work out the mechanics of sharing finances, doing chores and parental responsibilities. The concept of an economic partnership is the basis of matrimonial law as it applies to relationship breakdowns. The rules vary by jurisdiction, but one common aspect of family law is an even splitting of assets acquired during the marriage. The legislation will outline how the assets are to be split, but it is common to allow couples to opt out of the rules by entering into a domestic contract, sometimes called a marriage contract. There are normally restrictions on what can be contained in the contract, such as issues related to the custody of children and special rules may apply to the matrimonial home.

Couples often cannot agree on either the need for a contract or the details it should contain. There appears to be a greater use of domestic contracts in second marriages when one party wants to ensure certain assets are protected for the benefit of the children of a former marriage. Perhaps the best perspective on this issue is to understand that legislation will provide a formula of how assets are to be divided upon separation. If the couple does not like the rules laid out in the legislation, they can choose their own formula. However, in many cases the legislative option is followed as either the couple could not agree on a better formula or the negotiation between the spouses became heated and it was not possible to reach an agreement.

The circumstances of the relationship can also impact the motivation to enter a domestic contract. A couple, who marries in their twenties and have approximately equal assets may find a 50/50 split reasonable. Besides being twenty-five and in love, they both know their love will last forever. A couple in their sixties who are entering second marriages may have acquired unequal assets and bring a lifetime of experience to the table. At least one of the potential spouses may desire a contract. However, these negotiations may be painful, since both spouses should be represented by legal counsel throughout the process.

Consider the example of a couple in their fifties who have decided to enter into a second marriage for both parties. The gentleman has significant wealth, while his future bride had a modest level of assets. The wedding date has been set and the contract negotiations appear to be moving ahead in a civil and respectful manner. The gentleman was deeply in love and after years of an unhappy marriage, he believes the future is bright. He is a very successful and sophisticated businessman, while his future wife has a modest job and overflows with charm and personality. Everyone loved her and were so happy that they found each other. Then eight weeks before the date of the wedding, the future bride launched the nuclear option. She told the love of her life that she wanted to marry him, but she was not going to sign a domestic contract or enter into any further negotiations. There was a veiled threat that if the marriage did not go forward, living in a common-law relationship was not an option she would consider. He had the choice of canceling the marriage or going forward without a contract. The gentleman had many sleepless nights, but he relented and they married without a contract. In this battle between the brain the heart, the heart won and they were married on the date that had been previously announced. They had a lovely marriage and were able to enjoy the fruits of a successful relationship for about eleven years. Then something happened as the romance and the marriage ended. Not everyone lives happily ever after.

As individuals age, there is a reduction in their sexual currency, which may explain the amount of age discrimination in our society. When individuals over the age of fifty lose their job, it is incredibly difficult to find employment at a similar salary as their former job. We understand that libido can decline with age, but it also applies to sexual currency in the job market.

Is there a connection between diversity and sexual currency? The answer is no since sexual currency is the advantage achieved by an attractive appearance and charisma, while diversity provides an economic advantage because one was born with a vagina or darker skin pigmentation.

Social Capital

Social capital refers to the network of people with whom we have a connection. They can provide advice, contacts and help each other out. A simplistic example would be neighbors who watch each other's home when the families are on vacation. This is an example of friends helping friends. However, our focus is on the economic side of social capital, which is the ability to achieve a financial advantage because of relationships. Certain ethnic cultures have practiced this art for years. They go to the same church and support each other's businesses. Social capital is not about having a thousand friends on Facebook, nor is it about knowing important people. It is using these contacts to achieve some financial advantage. The wealthy have an easier time making these connections because they can join private clubs or non-profit boards with like-minded people. Partners in legal and accounting firms can often open doors with just a phone call. Many successful people cultivate such relationships and use it to their advantage. Most companies, industries and cities have power brokers. It is not enough to just identify these rainmakers, but devise a concise answer to the question - why should they help me? These connections can create opportunities that many people never know existed. A classic strategy used by wealthy families to increase the social capital of their children is to place them in expensive private schools. Connections are often made in these schools that last a lifetime.

A secondary type of social capital refers to the social skills that a person possesses. Most parents try to teach manners to the children although the advice may be rudimentary, such as do not eat with your fingers or don't stab your sister with the fork. A lack of these skills can limit advancement within a firm and this is an advantage that may accrue to children of upper-income families. If hosting clients is a component of the job, a lack of social skills can limit advancement or kill a career. Etiquette can be taught, but it is a much more complex as to how parents can help their children develop leadership skills, empathy, gravitas and charisma.

Bottom Line - It does not seem fair that looks and charisma can provide financial advantages or wealthy unattractive men marry beautiful women. Life is not fair and this will never change.

CHAPTER SEVENTEEN

INSTITUTIONS

The harder I work, the luckier I get

It easy to make a normative statement as to what governments, institutions and businesses should do to restore the middle class to its former glory. However, there is an obvious flaw in this approach, as institutions will continue to carry out the mandate of their existence, which means looking after their best interests. Companies emphasize maximizing profits; while governments focus on retaining power. It is naïve to expect them to act in any other manner. We have many powerful institutions in our society including businesses, unions and educational institutions, that could take steps to help the middle class, but with the exception of governments that is not their mission.

There is little an individual can do to make a significant impact on society. However, institutions can drive change. Usually making suggestions what others can do to improve our lot in life is time well wasted, but let's charge into the abyss. Institutions are well aware of the value of the services they provide, but as the boomer generation fades into the dark, they must examine their role in a world of increased income inequality. It is easy to continue offering the same service to a shrinking middle class and ignore the needs of the expanding underclass. If

118

institutions choose to address the needs of the less prosperous segments of society, there are a number of issues to be considered. Can post-secondary schools ensure their students graduate with skills valued by employers, while not being excessively burdened by student loans? Should businesses continue to focus on maximizing profit, or do they take a more nationalistic view of the economy? This could include keeping high-paying jobs at home, but it is problematic if their competitors utilize cheap foreign labor. This strategy would have a higher degree of success if consumers were prepared to pay higher prices for products manufactured in their home country.

Educational Institutions

A strength of our Western civilization is our world class universities. They have done a phenomenal job of fulfilling their mandate by turning out highly trained and successful graduates. World-class professors and research facilities attract students from around the globe. Our larger schools have evolved from ivy-covered buildings to small cities that can provide almost any service a student requires without leaving campus. Despite the positives of these fine institutions, this is the first generation that is questioning whether or not a university education is a good investment. There is a fear of facing a job market that does not embrace their skills while being saddled with a significant debt load. The cost of a university degree has risen dramatically and we are expecting teenagers, who are not always the most informed thinkers, to decide if they will receive a reasonable rate of return on an investment in higher education. This raises four questions:

1. Should universities provide an education or should they expand their mission and focus on

119

ensuring their graduates possess skills that are valued in the workplace?

2. Do universities have any responsibility to make higher education affordable or should be they be allowed to continue their level of spending and pass the costs onto students?

3. Large universities have been able to insulate themselves from various disruptive technologies that could drive down the cost of education. Should they be forced to change their business model since it is working so well?

4. Is it time to reconsider the professor-student relationship? Professors may consult, perform research and work with graduate students but may not spend a lot of time at the front of the lecture hall.

It would be ideal if all graduates acquired a valuable skill and post-secondary education was more affordable. Not all courses are designed to provide a recognized skill nor are they equal when it comes to landing a job. Schools correctly argue that students choose the courses; they just provide a menu from which the student can select. The problem is that the high-value degrees such as engineering and business tend to fill up quickly, but there is usually space in courses on women studies and children's literature. The schools are also correct that not all students could graduate with a science or law degree and they need courses available for the less gifted students. In the 60s and 70s, there was a sexist expression known as a "marriage degree." Young women could go to school, take easy courses and land a mate, as opposed to the current day when enrolling in college is the first step to running the world. A liberal arts degree has been referred to as the "dummy track" or the "party path," but for many, it is "Last Chance U." It has become the default degree for many students who do not get accepted in their top choices or lack the skills to graduate from the more difficult programs.

Universities do not have incentives to be cost efficient. American schools may pay football coaches salaries that may be in the millions of dollars while hiring thousands of administrators and building enormous structures. It appears they want to be a world unto themselves.

Let's take a take a look at some totally hypothetical numbers at a prestigious university. Our assumptions are:

- Tuition is $25,000, which does not include a few thousand dollars of compulsory charges, such as student fees, bus passes and use of athletic facilities.
- First-year students take five courses and our hypothetical student is enrolled in political science, so we assume the cost is $5,000 per course.
- First-year courses may have a class size of more than 500 students. Class size will drop significantly for those enrolled in classes in subsequent years.
- Students receive three lectures per week. If the course provides excellent teaching notes, it may not be necessary to attend every class. This is especially true if the classes start at 8:30 am.
- Since it is a first-year course, it is taught by an associate professor. Essays and exams are marked by teaching assistants who are working on their doctorate.

Let's look at a hypothetical income statement for this course:

University Revenue
    500 students @ $5,000 $2,500,000

University Expenses
    Lecturer at $100 per hour - assume $ 10,800

    Time for office meetings   unknown

    Overhead - classroom, supplies etc.   unknown

    Profit   well over $2 million

Note - A good accountant could reduce the profit on these courses by recharging additional expenses such as a portion of the football coach's salary, the cost of new dorms and a portion of the dean's residence.

There is no issue that class size and tuition differ significantly between universities, but Fortune 500 companies would be jealous of this profit margin, especially on first-year liberal art courses. As class size decreases, the profit per class drops significantly. It becomes obvious why universities promote liberal arts courses. They claim it is because it enhances critical thinking skills, teaches the student to think for themselves, communicate effectively or whatever. These are skills that almost every student acquires whether the degree is in law, engineering or the history of Europe in the middle ages. These arguments are frequently advanced by liberal arts departments. Are 500 people traveling to a large hall for a lecture the best use of technology? Universities claim to be teaching the latest in technology so why not give the students access to all the lectures on electronic media? Whether it is available for download or passed out at the start of the year, introducing disruptive technologies could significantly decrease the cost of certain university courses. This cost reduction strategy will work much better in liberal arts courses than the more demanding courses such as engineering, medicine or the sciences.

If these massive/obscene profit margins were reduced, tuition and student debt could be reduced accordingly. Until there is an incentive for universities to reduce costs, do not expect any change. Significant cost reduction can result if universities cut back on their lavish spending on facilities and services. They could also rethink the allocation of their teaching staff's time. How many hours should be spent teaching vs. assisting doctorate students? Is the "publish or perish" concept outdated and should it apply to all faculties, especially the liberal arts? Is it important that a professor specializing in medieval poetry spend a significant amount of time publishing and performing research? Should professors in the MBA program be allowed to consult and keep a share of the profits? Do tenured professors have to meet certain expectations, or is there an element of compensation for services rendered in previous years?

Universities have numerous opportunities to reduce the cost of an education. Training a student to be a doctor will always be expensive, but it is unfortunate that graduates with few recognizable skills should incur such costs. Would it be a bad idea if we had less liberal arts slots available while increasing number of science, math and engineering graduates? This would make graduating university more challenging as some students lack the academic strength to succeed in the more challenging courses.

Companies understand that if an expense is incurred, it is included in the price that customers pay to purchase the product. If the product becomes too expensive customers may go elsewhere. This is not an issue for top universities since if students want to obtain a degree, they have no choice but to pay the going rate and their pricing model appears to be charge what the market will bear. The best students will seek out the best universities, regardless of cost. Some MBA degrees cost more than $100,000. Certainly, there are degrees that cost significantly less, such as women's studies. This may be an example of getting what we pay for.

Post-secondary schools are incredible institutions that turn out well-educated leaders of tomorrow. But if expenses are going to be reduced to make higher education more affordable, it will be imposed on them externally as there is no internal impetus to make the necessary changes.

The cost of a higher education can also be addressed through government actions. Options include free tuition or student loan forgiveness. Unfortunately, these are expensive options in a period of ongoing deficits. Universities have no incentive to be cost effective. They build dorms that are like hotels, world class sports facilities and employ well-paid administers to perform various jobs. They may have bus systems, campus police and medical facilities. Many universities are self-sufficient small cities.

Secondary schools could also do a better job of preparing students who may be classified as non-academics. As many students, especially boys, continue to underperform in school, it may be time to consider changing our school system to a more non-academic friendly environment. Math and science are not for everyone and consideration should be given to introducing a stronger vocational system. This will aid young men who lack interest in math and science and allow them to focus on skills more consistent with their abilities. In high school, we were required to study a Shakespearian play each year. Although he was a great author, it was clear most of us would never read another play after graduation. We were taught theoretical concepts such as trigonometry, geometry, algebra and calculus which was important for those taking certain courses in university, but some students had trouble making change from a dollar. We were not taught financial planning, how to perform CPR, understanding mental health issues or relating to people who were different than us. Gifted children will fly through the academic side of high school, but there is a segment of the student body that struggles, perhaps because of less than average IQ, disinterest, or issues at home that leave them unprepared to face the daily grind of school. If these students enter the world with only a high school degree and no marketable skills, we have set them up for failure. It is better to invest in their education while attending school than funding their lifestyle as an underemployed member of the underclass. There are issues concerning streaming students at an early age which is well understood within the academic community, but access to vocational programs can be an important option in a student's career.

Business

America is the leader in the art of capitalism and their world class companies have created wealth for shareholders and employees. They have developed new technologies in fields from medicine to computers and have raised the quality of life not only in America but around the world. Their taxes fund the finest military the world has ever seen and it created an environment where anyone could achieve a level of success regardless of the income of their parents. With their wealth and power, two questions arise concerning the role of business in our society:

1. Is the primary purpose of a corporation to maximize profit? If one agrees with this theory, then moving jobs offshore, polluting the environment and lobbying the government to reduce consumer protection should be fair game.

2. Should a corporation be nationalist and put the interests of the home country above the profit maximization doctrine?

Assume a manufacturing plant that pays $30 per hour can be relocated offshore and employees can be replaced by foreign workers who earn a few dollars per day. If a product was sold exclusively in South America, then moving a plant from Los Angeles to Mexico may be reasonable in the circumstances. However, if the products are sold exclusively in California, does it make sense to move the manufacturing facilities from Los Angeles to Mexico City and export the products into California? The company has created additional wealth, but shutting factories may have destroyed the lifestyle of many families. It is unfair to generalize as many companies take their corporate responsibilities quite seriously. However, if CEOs believe their job may be in jeopardy if profits decline, then following the herd and focusing on cost reduction will increase profitability and probably lengthen their tenure with the company. The same as a bike racer who uses steroids, because if competitors are on the juice and the cyclist does not follow suit, winning is out of the question. A change to the profit maximization philosophy may not be an ideology that emerges from within the corporate world. Many corporations are citizens of the world with subsidiaries in many countries. Why should they maximize the position of employees in their home country, when they have employees and customers around the world? If the government tries to force the hand of big business to act in a more nationalistic manner, what is the outcome when these two goliaths collide? Normally in such cases, the corporations win and the politicians declare victory.

Should companies be nationalistic and owe some economic debt to the country in which they were incorporated? This is not an issue for companies that only sell within their borders, but if companies have customers and plants around the globe, where should their loyalties lie? The current corporate thinking appears to be that a company's primary concerns are their shareholders and customers. Many companies are committed to being good corporate citizens in the countries in which they operate. However, maximizing profit may mean reducing labor costs by shifting jobs overseas. What incentives are available for companies to keep jobs at home where wages are higher and labor issues are more complex? When faced with the option of closing three plants, laying off 5,000 workers and moving the jobs offshore to maximize profit, how wonderful it would be if the CEO said "screw the extra profits, my country and workers are more important." Such a CEO may be a local hero, but he may also be forced to seek employment elsewhere in the near future. This home country first mentality can only be successful if consumers are prepared to pay a higher price for these products. Unfortunately, too many consumers want manufacturing jobs to remain in the country but demand lower prices. When they vote with their wallet, nothing will change.

Bottom Line - Although educational institutions and business may be able to take steps to strengthen the middle class, that is not why they exist. They will continue to do what they have always done to achieve their objectives, except they will get better at it. As for the fate of the middle class, this is not their issue.

CHAPTER EIGHTEEN

JOBS WITH A SHORT SHELF LIFE

*When you make a mistake, fall on your sword
and make no excuses*

Imagine being appointed general manager of your favorite major-league baseball team. It has not been in the playoffs for six years, but the farm team is well stocked with good young prospects. Since there are thirty teams in the league, all things being equal (and they are never equal) a team should expect to win the World Series approximately once every thirty years.

An evaluation of the competition suggests that your team plays in a strong division and the short-term outlook is not optimistic. There are two options to build a winner. The best strategy is to have a billionaire owner who wants to win at all costs and has no interest in the bottom line. Buying the services of the best players should produce wins and as a byproduct, the owner will be a major celebrity in the city. This could be called the Steinbrenner strategy. When this option is not available and there is no access to unlimited amounts of cash, the team may follow the classic rebuild strategy:

- Poor results lead to high draft picks and it is important to sign the top players selected.

128

- At the trade deadline, move higher-priced veteran players for prospects from other teams.
- In the offseason, refuse to sign over-priced free agents that are approaching the end of their career, but still demand top dollar for their declining skills.
- Invest in an excellent scouting system with an emphasis on the Caribbean, Asia and South America.
- Develop a world class analytics department.

One does not have to be Brian Cashman or Billy Beane to understand this is the classic strategy for long-term success. However, it helps to have the expertise of Cashman or Beane to know which players to draft. Most general managers agree this is an appropriate strategy and in five to six years a team can be fielded that can compete with the best in baseball. However, five more years of not making the playoffs may result in dropping attendance, alienating fans and ownership is reconsidering who can best fill the role of general manager.

The shelf life of a typical general manager may be in the four to six-year range, but if the team has not made the playoffs since being hired, one should not expect a long tenure. In other words, if developing a long-term plan is measured on short-term results, the plan may never be implemented since the general manager will be replaced by someone who understands the win-now philosophy. In other words, do the right thing, lose your job.

The life of a general manager has a certain glamor aspect, as his picture is frequently in the newspaper and he is constantly quoted in the press. It is cool to be a celebrity in a major-league sport and there are perks available that were never imagined when the job was offered, plus the salary provides a great lifestyle for the family. If the objective is not to get fired, then winning games becomes important. As a result, the rebuild plan is thrown away and the team signs free agents and trades the crown jewels of the farm system. This will increase the probability of winning immediately and extend his tenure but at the cost of a long-term strategy that has a legitimate chance of building a winner. The team may win more than it loses, but may never get past the first round of the playoffs. The result is the team does not win the World Series, the general manager gets fired, but being a professional baseball general manager was the ride of his life.

Short-term thinking is not limited to sports, as the same concept applies to business and government. Let's review the short shelf life theory as it applies to the chief executive officer of large corporations. The tenure of this position continues to shorten and if CEOs wants to maintain their job, sales and profits have to grow at a rate that satisfies the market. If the company has exciting new technologies, rapid growth may be possible. However, many companies have mature products in competitive markets, so if economies are growing by 1-2% per year, profitable growth is a challenge.

The CEO receives an excellent compensation package that may include a lucrative bonus and stock options that can provide obscene amounts of cash, especially if the stock market is rising. Our CEO is in a similar short-term predicament as the baseball general manager. By delivering profits that exceed the market's expectations; he can maintain his job and earn an income on the same level as rock stars and professional athletes. Growing a profitable business involves investments in training, new product development and research. If a CEO cannot grow sales, he can still increase profit by cutting costs at a faster rate than the increase in sales. He can deliver profits and protect his tenure by taking actions such as:

- Cut employment levels and put a freeze on hiring.
- Move the manufacturing offshore to reduce labor costs.
- Slash spending on research and new product development.
- Use available cash to buy back shares, rather than invest in new plants and equipment.
- Raise the dividend as this tends to increase the value of the shares and coincidentally the value of the CEO's stock options.

If the purpose of the corporation is to maximize profits, these steps will increase profits in the short-term and maximize the CEO's compensation. His efforts may produce excellent short-term results for the company and the executive team, but not for the community, the workers who lost their jobs or the long-term health of the company. The CEO understood the potential short shelf life of his position, so he implemented a strategy that increased his job security while maximizing short-term profit.

Just as the general manager and CEO may have a brief tenure if they do not deliver results in the short-term, the same results may apply to our political leaders. Once elected to lead a government, the next election is just a few years in the future. Despite every good intention of serving their constituents and doing what is best for the country, leaders understand they must face the electorate in a few years and will be judged by their performance in office. Even though they may have inherited a large debt and many departments have out of control spending, options are often measured by its impact on the next election campaign. Given the potential shelf life of a politician; is introducing an austerity budget to benefit our children or continue stimulus spending and supporting the needs of special interest groups provide the greatest chance of re-election? Most governments will stick to the short-term formula that has worked so well in the past. The standard strategy includes:

- Continue to emphasize fundraising and stay true to the financial backers who were responsible for the previous election victory.
- Politics has evolved into a permanent campaign and all policy initiatives must be viewed in light of their impact on the next election. Doing the right thing and losing the next election is not today's political reality.
- Do not address the debt issue by cutting spending as this tactic will increase noise from groups that received reduced funding.
- Always claim there is a plan to eliminate the deficit and balance the budget. Claim that government's initiatives will increase economic activity and result in additional tax revenue. Pay lip service to controlling costs and reducing corruption. Repeat this mantra every year.
- If government workers demand higher wages, take the necessary steps to avoid labor disruptions. The public will demand services and if the unions organize against the government, it can negatively impact the re-election bid.
- Talk of ethics and integrity, but when there is an ethical violation the leader must claim accountability and ensure the term is hollow by having no legitimate consequences.
- Continue to make speeches stating that economic growth is the government's highest priority and argue that all economic setbacks

are the result of global forces beyond the government's control.

Politicians know in their heart that increased spending and ongoing deficits will hurt our children and future generations, but let this be a problem for their successors. This strategy tends to keep politicians in power even if means acting as a financial pedophile.

Problems that took years to develop, often take years to fix. If politicians are primarily concerned with retaining power, it is reasonable to expect rhetoric, rather than making tough decisions that may be politically unpopular.

Bottom Line - In almost every field of endeavor, long-term results may never be achieved if short-term considerations impact the career and compensation of decision makers. When politics, power and levels of compensation are pitted against doing the right thing, should we be surprised at the course of action chosen by our leaders? Baseball general managers, CEOs and political leaders seldom remain in their positions for over a decade, but what a ride they had while it lasted.

They Keynesian economic theory of running deficits in difficult economic times and surpluses in periods of prosperity appears to have been replaced by perpetual deficits. Prime Minister Thatcher noted that the problem with socialism is that eventually you run out of other people's money. This ongoing deficit strategy appears to be best for the governing party despite the cost to future generations.

CHAPTER NINETEEN

OUTLIERS

When you are on a team, your primary objective is to be the best teammate you can be

Flashback to a statistics course from your student days and remember the bell curve. It shows the distribution of some variable. The highest point on the curve is the most probable event in the data and other possible occurrences are equally distributed around the top of the curve. The middle of the graph, or top of the bell, is the mean point and there are an equal number of data points on both sides. As a result, the graph is shaped like a bell. As a hypothetical example, we could plot the average salary of every male in the United States. The mean may be $50,000 and the further to the right on the graph we move, the higher the salary, but fewer people are making that level of income. As a result, the slope of the graph declines. On the extreme right of the graph may be Tim Cook or Tom Brady's salary, while on the extreme left there may be a homeless person who lives on government assistance.

We shall focus on the bell curve as it applies to the ranking of an individual's skills, rather than numerical measures such as salary. The most competent experts would be on the extreme right of the bell curve, while the most inept would be on the extreme left. Most people would be lumped in the middle and would be considered about average. There are four components of the bell curve that are relevant to our discussion:

1. Outliers - Outliers are the extremes at either end of the bell curve. They are the exceptions and the furthest from being average.
2. Phenomenal 1% - This refers to the stars at the extreme right of the bell curve. They are the elite of their profession and they are the best of the best.
3. The bottom 20% - This refers to the poor performers in the group. Other than in seniority based organizations, they are the most vulnerable to job loss.
4. Corrupt 1% - This is the extreme bottom and they may suffer from incompetence, a lack of personal integrity or outright corruption.

Typically, we deal with individuals that are more or less average in their skill set. It is uncommon to come across the phenomenal 1%, as they are rare and incredibly expensive. Dealing with the bottom 20% can result in service levels that are below our expectations while encountering the corrupt 1% can be downright dangerous.

When Jack Welch was CEO of General Electric, he introduced a performance ranking system known as the vitality curve. However, employees called it other names, such as rank and yank or much worse. In this system, the bottom 10% were fired. When Welch retired, he was replaced by Jeffrey Immelt and he eliminated this ranking system and eventually moved to abolish the annual performance appraisal. This move was praised by employees around the world, except human resource departments who saw their expertise being devalued. Since GE was considered a company with a strong management team, other companies copied their practices from rank and yank to Six Sigma, but with some modifications. For example, some companies attempted to identify the bottom 20% and if employees received this ranking for two years in a row, they could be fired. Enron, which was the poster child for the greed and fear mentality, had a 1 - 5 ranking with one being the highest. The corporate procedure required 15% of staff to be classified with a ranking of five. They had two weeks to find another job in the company or be fired.

It is reasonable to identify a company's weakest performers, but these systems had a devastating impact on morale, plus managers became adept at protecting favorite employees. The irony is that GE hired high performers and paid their employees very well. Many of their weakest performers may be stars in other companies. As soon as a company fires the bottom 10%, by definition, it is replaced by a new bottom 10% that will be vulnerable in next year's performance review.

Measurement of an individual's skills can be problematic. Very few functions in the workforce are measurable with a high degree of precision and there will always be a subjective component in the ranking. Sales reps are expected to attain a forecast and data entry staff can have their input measured, but many measurements can be manipulated. Should a worker on an assembly line work as fast as possible or a police officer be judged on the number of traffic tickets issued? Qualitative assessments are subjective. An employee could receive a high rating on a performance appraisal, but if the individual gets a new boss, the rating could change even though the work output is constant. This could be the result of the manager not liking the employee's style or possibly the application of different standards and expectations. Many companies attempt to minimize these issues by basing performance appraisals on meeting some predetermined objectives.

Regardless of the techniques used to measure the competencies of its staff, the skill sets will form a bell curve with high achievers on one end and poor performers on the weak end of the bell curve. Every large group will have a bottom 20%, even if there is not full agreement on the accuracy of the measuring process. Just because employees are in the bottom 20% does not necessarily mean they are performing their job below expectations. For example, assume an investment bank added ten Harvard MBAs, all of which were in the top 20% of their class, to a new trading department. When their first performance appraisal is completed, two of these ten new hires will be in the bottom 20% of the group, even if they are exceeding their employer's expectations. If the company has some rank and yank performance appraisal system, the two fired employees may land at a competitor and within a year could be two top guns in the new company. Thus, being in the bottom 20% does not necessarily mean the individuals are poor performers, it depends upon the competency of the staff and the measurement systems.

In a large group of employees, there will be a bottom 20% of performers and they may or may not meet the standards of the job. It is just a fact of life that some employees are weaker than others and in a ranking system, someone has to be at the bottom. Within the bottom 20%, there is a very small subgroup of individuals that are corrupt, grossly incompetent, predators, or downright evil. There are very bad people in our society and although some are in prison, others are priests, soldiers, teachers and CEOs. Some are sociopaths looking for opportunities for financial gain or sexual gratification. They may or may not be competent at their job, but they will use the power of their position to carry out a personal agenda. Their victim may be someone's child, spouse or bank account. It would seem reasonable that once they are discovered, they would be fired from the job and their activities would be reported to the authorities. In reality, there are three common scenarios:

- The individual's activities are identified and there is an appropriate response that may include termination, criminal charges or expulsion from the organization.
- The human contaminate is not identified and may continue his evil ways.
- Once the activities of the individual are known, no action is taken because of either institutional corruption or the employee is represented by a union or an employee association that restricts the employer's ability to dismiss individuals without a long and costly due process.

Recently three friends advised that a family member was scheduled for a major operation. As part of the small talk surrounding the upcoming hospitalization, all three mentioned how fortunate they were to have the best surgeon in the city performing the operation. This raises the question – how did they know who the best surgeon was? Perhaps the referring doctor commented on the skill set of the surgeon to put the patient at ease, or it could have been a neighbor or the local postal carrier that provided the information. Perhaps the surgeon was best in class thirty years ago and survives on a reputation that is no longer warranted.

At a convention of surgeons, a speaker posed a question to his audience, which consisted of surgeons from the country's major hospitals. The question – If you know a fellow surgeon that is working in your hospital that you would not allow operating on a family member; would you please raise your hand? Apparently, everyone in the room raised their hand.

We have a disconnect, as patients, we have a high level of confidence in the ability of our surgeon, yet there are doctors who should not have operating room privileges and the layperson cannot tell the difference. When we hire a professional, our lives are literally in their hands and selecting the appropriate professional is of paramount importance. We want our advisors to be of the top shelf variety, but we tend to judge them on a combination of charisma, the level of service provided, or the opinion of a third party who probably has no expertise on the topic.

When we refer to the bottom 20%, we mean those individuals whose skill set is significantly less than average. They may be good people and try their best, but some people are just not cut out for certain jobs. It can be work ethic, aptitude, desire, age, addiction, intelligence or any number of factors can result in an individual being a subpar performer. Some organizations identify these individuals and attempt to rectify the problem through retraining or moving them to a position more suitable to their skill set. Employers normally know the identity of their weakest links, but due to labor laws, union representation or a lack of gonads, they are allowed to carry on. If the low-performing individual is a customer service rep for the cable company that messes up a service call, it is marginally upsetting, but life goes on. However, if the weak performer is the lawyer hired to defend your son on an impaired driving charge or the surgeon who is performing hip replacement surgery on your spouse, the consequences can be life changing.

Misuse of the Outliers Concept - An outlier can also be used in an attempt to discredit the average or middle of the bell curve. For example, renowned scientists have made statements in good faith that have later proved to be wrong. Thus, arguments are presented against the theory that humans played a part in global warming because science has been wrong before. The intelligence community was wrong on the issue of whether or not Saddam Hussein had weapons of mass destruction. This convinces some to believe that intelligence reports can never be trusted since they have been erroneous in the past.

Bottom Line - In every aspect of life one should attempt to identify those top performers and attempt to avoid the bottom 20%. Unfortunately, most people believe they can tell the difference by listening to a third-party endorsement or rating charisma. The elite 1% are normally known in the community and are very expensive and difficult to retain, whereas the corrupt 1% are problematic to identify. In an upcoming chapter on selecting advisors, we shall review strategies to avoid these bottom feeders.

Anytime an individual is seeking to hire, attend school, marry or seek the counsel of a professional, seek out that elite 1% or at least as close as your skill set or finances will allow. It is one issue to have a connection with the elite 1%, but quite another to maintain the relationship as they may have higher expectations than the norm. Many unsophisticated people understand the need to select those at the strong end of the bell curve, but often they rely on the advice of friends and family who have no expertise and may be totally uninformed. This strategy of the blind leading the blind tends not to optimize potential outcomes and many that inadvertently utilize this strategy are often unaware of the price they paid or the opportunities that may have been lost.

CHAPTER TWENTY

COUNSEL

If you want something done, give it to a busy person

There is a story of Joe Kennedy, the patriarch of a very rich and powerful family. One son became a president, two others became senators and the family fascinated the public for years. In 1929, the stock market was rising and the roaring twenties were still going strong. As the legend goes, Mr. Kennedy stopped for a shoe shine and while he was getting buffed and polished, the shoeshine boy dispensed some stock advice. He had some hot tips and enjoyed sharing them with his clients. Mr. Kennedy thanked the young man and went about his business. However, the young man's advice stuck in his mind and he asked himself the following question - if shoeshine boys are making money in the market, are stocks overvalued? According to the legend, Mr. Kennedy liquidated most of his investments. Shortly after that, the stock market crashed and the Kennedy fortune remained intact. How much of this story is literally true may be disputed, but the message is obvious. As my brilliant, but intimidating marketing professor stated, you do not become wise, by hearing wise men say wise things. Without taking action, wisdom is wasted.

Selecting Professionals

Purchasing advice from professionals is a key component of a successful financial plan and the process to select advisors is straightforward, often as the result of a recommendation from a friend. A phone call is made, an appointment is scheduled and the relationship begins. Now compare this process to companies seeking to hire an accounts payable clerk. They gather resumes, conduct multiple interviews, perform background checks and interview references. After consultation with other senior employees, a selection is made. It may or may not make sense to put as much time and energy into selecting advisors as companies invest in the hiring process for entry level employees, but our time investment should be measured in hours, rather than seconds. Is the person that recommended a specific advisor competent to provide informed input? Many recommendations are based on ratings of service and charisma, rather than technical expertise. The best source of information is often derived from someone that works in the industry.

Most advisors are competent. The goal is to select those who are on the right end of the bell curve and avoid those who are significantly below average especially the corrupt 1%. The skills and competency of all professionals in a given field, such as law or medicine, could theoretically be ranked on a bell curve. As outlined in the chapter on outliers, the goal is to retain an advisor as close as possible to the elite 1% and avoid the bottom 20%. Below this threshold is incompetent and corrupt individuals that populate every line of work and it is critical to avoid these scoundrels.

An unsophisticated family needs to have a will prepared and selects a lawyer who is an alcoholic and is constantly fighting with the bar association to retain his right to practice law. Based on the advice of a well-intentioned but totally uninformed friend, the lawyer was contacted.

Preparing a will is a no brainer and assuming the will states the client's wishes, almost any lawyer in the world could draft a standard will, including a lawyer who is slightly inebriated. The lawyer selected may have been in the bottom 20%, but since he was recommended by a hair stylist and his work seems legit, we have a satisfied client. For all the client knows, the draft document could have been downloaded from the internet and omits most of the standard clauses contained in a will. The family may recommend this lawyer to a friend. Assume their son was driving a car while impaired and caused an accident which resulted in a death. Since they were happy with the will prepared by the marginally sober lawyer, he was retained to defend their son. This decision may result in a life sentence.

Similarly, if stitches are needed for a minor wound, the goal is to get immediate medical assistance. Not a time to pick and choose a medical provider who is considered the best in his field, as almost anyone can perform this service. However, if major heart surgery is required and the opportunity exists to have the operation done in a small-town hospital by a new doctor who has just arrived from overseas a few months ago, it might be best to determine if there are other available options.

Most professionals are competent, but there are exceptions. To receive excellent service and reduce the possibility of significant financial or personal loss from using the services of a substandard, corrupt or incompetent professional, consider the following guidelines when dealing with professionals.

Legal - On most crime dramas on television, the police arrested the suspected villain who turns to his wife and says "call my lawyer." If the police arrive at your door and the services of a lawyer are required immediately, would your family know who to call? If the police suspect that your son has been driving impaired and left the scene of an accident, it can be problematic if your lawyer is a one-person firm who closed your last home purchase. The lawyer's hours are 9:00 am to 5:00 pm and he may be impossible to reach at midnight. If it is possible to contact him, there may be some incredibly bad luck waiting, as the real estate lawyer may agree to defend your son. Hopefully, he will recommend another lawyer, but whether the recommendation is the best criminal lawyer in the city or his buddy, who has tried a few cases, remains an unknown. There is one question that everyone should ask their legal advisor. If a family member gets into legal trouble, in the evening or the weekend it is important to know who to call, regardless of the time.

Each large city has a number of top-shelf law firms. If individuals have a major legal issue, they should hire the best advice they can afford. Large firms not only have specialists in most areas of law, but they have internal procedures to ensure clients receive proper representation. If one is dealing with a routine legal transaction such as a house purchase or the preparation of a will, a small firm may offer a significant price advantage. However, for those that have been criminally charged or are being sued for negligence, this is no time to hire a generalist in an attempt to save a few bucks.

Using the services of a large law firm with specialists in most areas of the law will ensure proper representation, but the legal bills will not be inexpensive and there is no guarantee the case will be won. One of the truths in law that many clients fail to comprehend is there is a high probability that a person will be found guilty for the simple reason that he committed the crime. Lawsuits will be lost because the facts support the position of the opponent. Thus, one of the most important questions that can be asked of a lawyer is the probability of victory. Guilty people with expensive lawyers go to jail, just less often than guilty individuals who cannot afford the best and the brightest. When a guilty person is found innocent in a jury trial, it can reinforce the public's perception that there is one set of rules for the rich and another for the poor. The guilty are normally convicted, but the chances of being found innocent or having the sentence reduced are greatly increased by using the services of a best in class lawyer.

In addition to very large firms that cover most legal issues, there are boutique firms that specialize in specific areas of the law, such as criminal, family law or civil litigation. These firms retain top lawyers, so it is not always true that the biggest firms provide the best legal advice. Both large firms and boutique firms can provide great representation, but they do not compete on price.

People do stupid things and although we can accept on a philosophical level there should be consequences for inappropriate behavior, people would rather not get caught or be convicted for their actions. When bad things happen, everyone should get legal counsel as soon as possible to ensure their rights are protected, even if the result is facing the consequences of a bad action. The objective is to minimize the time between when the police advise there is a problem and the first contact with a lawyer. A person who has a lawyer present at the police interrogation has a higher probability of a better outcome than one not represented by counsel.

I had the opportunity to have supper with an individual that is considered to be one of the country's best legal minds. He made the comment that in our community it is almost impossible for the police to charge an innocent person with a crime. Innocent means that the person did not commit the crime or lie to the police to hide the involvement of either himself or his friends. The guilty may be found innocent for any number of reasons, often for lack of evidence, but if individuals did nothing wrong, they are rarely charged. Unfortunately, this is not true in all jurisdictions around the world.

The bottom line is that if family members are on the wrong side of the law, it is imperative that they know how to obtain counsel as soon as possible. This does not suggest the accused should not bear the consequences of the action; rather everyone has the right to counsel; just ensure it is obtained quickly and with a competent criminal lawyer.

Taxes - Having spent most of my adult life working in the field of taxation, I offer the following as the best advice you may ever receive - don't screw with the tax man. They are professional, methodical and very good at collecting taxes. Many fine upstanding citizens who would never steal a bag of peanuts from Walmart or drive a vehicle after a second drink often have no hesitation cheating on their taxes. There are various convoluted thought processes that attempt to justify this behavior. Perhaps it is because everyone does it or it's just the government, so there is no real victim and besides, working people already pay too much in taxes compared to those takers who bleed the system dry. There is also a perception that the chances of getting caught are minimal. Depending upon the nature of the transaction, it may or may not be a criminal act and we are not talking about honest errors or ignorance of the law, but an action that the person knows is wrong and still does it.

Would friends or family members do any of the following?

- Offer to pay cash to get a reduced price and avoid the sales tax.
- Exaggerate the number of business miles driven to maximize a tax-free reimbursement.
- Pay cash for work performed to ensure the individual is not treated as an employee and thus avoid the various payroll taxes.
- Fail to report income received in cash such as tips or home renovation projects.

146

- Claim a personal expenditure, such as family dinner, as a business expense.
- Not declaring income received for day care services. Many sitters have two prices when they care for children. A higher price is charged that includes a receipt or a lower price with no receipts for payments in cash.
- Expensing a round of golf that was supposedly with a client, but was actually with a friend.

This list is endless and seems to be condoned by a large segment of the population. A tax auditor told the story of when auditing a small business, he always made small talk with the owner to a build a relationship. There are two pieces of information the auditor is attempting to acquire through the casual conversation. The auditor wants to know the dates of the spouse's birthday and their wedding anniversary. With the dates in hand, the auditor will eventually review expense reports to see if the business owner took a client out for dinner on those evenings. It is amazing how many times the owner went to a dinner at a romantic restaurant on his anniversary or wife's birthday. The auditor may call the guest who was supposedly at the dinner to confirm it was a business meal. All too often there was no client at the meal. As the auditor stated now we can start this audit and "I own his ass."

Investments – Receiving an adequate rate of return and not being overcharged on fees and commissions are common concerns of investors. It is annoying when recommended investments decline in value, but seldom does it wipe out an investor's portfolio. These are operational issues that can be addressed. The major concern is to avoid arrangements that could result in losing all your money through some type of fraud. Typically, the product purchased is significantly overvalued, the individual just takes the money and runs, or the investment turns out to be a Ponzi scheme. Losing a significant portion of one's wealth by relying on an unethical advisor is devastating. There are some steps that can be taken to eliminate or significantly reduce the possibility of being defrauded. These include:

- Always avoid unsolicited offers. Never buy an investment from a person or firm that makes contact by phone, email, text, or knocks on the front door. Typically, the investor is promised a rate of return that is higher than is available in the marketplace. It could be orange juice futures, gems, penny stocks or whatever and the explanation will be that certain unusual circumstances have arisen that present an excellent buying opportunity for those that get in early. The bottom line is that if the rate of return is guaranteed and above the borrowing rate, why does the seller have to call strangers to make the sale? Perhaps he should go to the bank and borrow tons of cash and buy the product himself since the rate of return is so high and the risk so low. When approached by an unknown investment sales rep, hang up the phone, delete the email or sic the dogs on him if he comes to the door. The bottom line is the seller may be a scam artist and any investor may be the sucker.
- Only use the investment services of large firms with branches in multiple cities. There are some excellent smaller firms but assume that very few investors are smart enough to identify the good from the bad. Dealing with Goldman Sachs, TD Bank, Edward Jones or Charles Schwab does not guarantee that the investments will receive a superior return, but there is almost no chance the advisor will take the money and run. If there is an

internal fraud, the firm will stand behind the investors unless they were in some way complicit.

- Federal governments provide protection for certain types of accounts. The United States has the Federal Deposit Insurance Corporation and Canada has the Canada Deposit Insurance Corporation. Learn the rules in your jurisdiction and only maintain cash accounts in institutions that are covered by the insurance. Don't take the word of the institution as government websites will list all of the banks and financial institutions that are covered.
- Be leery of free seminars, as it is normally followed by a sales pitch that is designed to separate investors from their money. Promises may be made concerning the secrets of real estate investments, or how to use futures to create wealth. Avoid free seminars as they are very persuasive and the product being pitched may or may not be a legitimate investment opportunity.
- Use the smell test on every possible investment. If the proposal seems too good to be true, it probably is, so walk away.
- If somebody offers the opportunity to get on the ground floor of an investment, don't bite. These snake oil salesmen often infiltrate church groups and cultural functions as there is a higher level of trust in these settings.
- Avoid being the victim of identity theft. There is a ton of material available on this topic. Familiarize yourself with the information and be smart.
- Ensure the advisor sends financial reports on a regular basis and challenge discrepancies to someone higher up in the organization.

- If an advisor suggests an investment outside of the current firm, this may be problematic.
- Gold digging has always been a part of our society, but internet dating has opened a new avenue for fraud. It may be easy to picture gold digging women preying on older gentlemen, but male gigolos also have their share of targets. They charm, they marry and leave the relationship in a few years with a boatload of money. Quite often, a bank account is wiped out, but no crime may have been committed since it was a gift from a person who was in love.
- When an individual has been defrauded, the victim should always file a police report.

Investing can be challenging, but many potential issues can be avoided if we can simply control our greed. Even though most of these fraudsters eventually get caught, the money is seldom recovered.

Bottom Line – Selecting the right advisors can make a world of difference in your financial decisions. As a general rule, you get what you pay for so hire the best within your price range.

CHAPTER TWENTY-ONE

Taxation

How many people on their deathbed wish they had spent just a couple of more days at the office?

Perhaps the most honest assessment of tax policy was made by Jean-Baptiste Colbert who served as the Minister of Finance during the reign of King Louis XIV of France. He said that the art of taxation consists of plucking the goose to obtain the largest amount of feathers with the least possible amount of hissing. One of the truths of taxation that is not openly acknowledged by our political leaders is that taxation should be considered voluntary. To rephrase, we have to pay taxes to someone, but we can choose the government that will be the recipient of our tax payments. All that is required to implement this strategy is to move between tax jurisdictions. Taxpayers have the option of leaving the country and relocating to a jurisdiction with lower tax rates. A person making $60,000 is not going to change residences to save $800 per year unless there are non-tax reasons for the move and the tax savings are a side benefit. However, if a person is making $60,000,000 per year there can be a strong incentive to move to a jurisdiction with lower tax rates. Changing locations is a significant event for individuals, but a standard business strategy for global companies. When corporations decide to build a plant in Alabama or Mexico City, they consider taxes, labor and the cost of energy.

When a corporation moves offshore to save taxes, there may be press coverage, but for the most part, the wealthy can relocate totally under the radar. The term tax exile is used to describe individuals who change countries of residency to reduce taxes. Perhaps the most famous examples were the British super bands of the 1960s and 1970s. They were making tons of money, but the top tax rate in England was approximated 95%. They could protest or move. The Beatles wrote a song called The Taxman and the lyrics indicated the taxman kept nineteen for himself and there was one left for you. It is unclear if the song had any impact on the eventual reduction in top rates, but many bands moved out of the reach of British tax authorities. The Rolling Stones moved to France in 1971 and then released the album Exile on Main Street, which reinforced the impact of taxation on their life. Mick Jagger and Keith Richards remain tax exiles and are only allowed to visit England for a limited number of days per year, or they will face a significant tax penalty. Apparently, taxes were the motivation for David Bowie moving to Switzerland, Ringo Star to Monte Carlo and Rod Stewart moving to California.

One of the more recent high-profile tax exiles was Eduardo Saverin who was one of the founders of Facebook. It is reported he owns over 50 million shares of the company and in 2011 he renounced his American citizenship and moved to Singapore. It has been estimated this move saved him more than 500 million dollars in taxes.

A plumber is not going change countries to save a few thousand dollars, but corporations and the wealthy can use the mobility of their capital to relocate to a more favorable tax jurisdiction. As a side benefit, most of these countries have a warmer climate.

Bottom Line - Achieve even reasonable success in life and you will pay over half your annual income in taxes. In addition to income taxes, there are property taxes, sales taxes and gasoline taxes. Invest the time to understand how to reduce your tax liability.

CHAPTER TWENTY-TWO

PROTESTS AND ACTIVISM

It is OK to glance at our past, just do not stare

The greatest generation kept to themselves, showed incredible patriotism and supported the police, but they often appeared blind to the struggle for equality for blacks, women and gays. Perhaps they were happy with the status quo and did not like people who were different than themselves. Racial insensitivity was commonplace in their language and it was not intended to offend, it was just the way they talked. Protests were rare and the police were intolerant of civil disobedience. Resolving the issues of transgender bathrooms would not be taken seriously by our grandparents.

Unlike the greatest generation, many boomers recognized injustices and formed alliances with the oppressed. They marched, sang protest songs and danced to music that outraged their parents. Students protested and they turned the 1968 Democratic Convention in Chicago into a war zone. The subsequent trial of the Chicago Seven challenged many principles that their parents had taken for granted. They were beaten, jailed, stopped a war and changed the country forever. The ideas that sprang from these protests changed our political system and we started down a road to address many aspects of social injustice.

It is a common topic of conversation comparing how boomers played as children compared to the current generation. We played outside with friends in activities that were unsupervised by adults, whereas many of today's youth play video games in the safety of their basement. Not only has the way kids play changed over time, but the important art of the protest has evolved in a similar manner. There were some protests as millennials came of age, such as the Occupy Movement or Black Lives Matter, but for the most part, these groups consisted of people that felt oppressed and there was minimal support from the middle class. However, many of our youth were prepared to support their causes on social media. Hitting the like button is a lot safer than civil obedience, but for a minimal contribution of their time, many believed they were helping the oppressed. Even if they did not want to protest outside their basement, they could send stories of injustice to their social media friends and share their outrage. This level of activism would make Jerry Rubin, Abbie Hoffman and Phil Ochs roll over in their graves.

Throughout the book, I have referred to the possibility of protests from angry working-class families and underemployed males. In 2011, there was a protest that started in New York known as Occupy Wall Street. In the original protest, one of the slogans was "We are the 99%," which was a reference to the one percent of the population that controls a significant portion of global wealth. They were protesting income inequality and the impact Wall Street firms were perceived to have on government policy. The demonstrations were a flashback to the traditional protests of the 1960s. The leaders believed they had a legitimate cause and the movement spread to many major cities around the world. However, professional protesters came out of hibernation and the crazies stepped forward to share their views on the end of money, the overthrow of capitalism and beauty of anarchy. Needless to say, it lost sight of the original goals and soon died out. This protest expressed the frustration felt by many working-class families, but it is not their nature to camp out in an attempt to eliminate injustice. These men and women want opportunities, but if there is no agreement on solutions, it is unclear how they will express their frustration. Protests come in many forms including marches, demonstrations, product boycotts, strikes and civil disobedience. These tactics can be very effective at raising levels of awareness, but they will not impose a resolution of these important issues, as there is no consensus on solutions. The legitimate exercise of free speech alone will not create opportunities for underemployed families.

It is difficult to predict how this anger will be expressed and whether any solutions will be effectively implemented. It is reasonable to expect ongoing outbursts of rage and support for populist movements that are more nationalistic and are not committed to free trade and the various forms of globalization. The term populist refers to political philosophies that relate to the concerns of working people. Those that are opposed to populism tend to define it as a philosophy that offers simplistic solutions to complex issues. The opposite of populism is elitism which may have two distinct meanings. The first is old money which consists of the upper crust of society. These are powerful and wealthy families that have significant influence in the nation's affairs. The term also refers to those who are well educated and politically active. This group often includes lawyers, business people, professors and numerous self-defined intellectuals. There is a sense among elitists that they are more knowledgeable than ordinary people and their opinions should carry a greater weight. In the United States, there is a rough geographical divide between the two philosophies, as the elitists are often located on the two coasts, while the strength of populism is in the traditional rust belt.

As the underclass acquires a critical mass, there will be an ongoing conflict between the populists and elitists. This is sometimes referred to as Main Street vs. Wall Street. The populist movement can be a top-down driven philosophy, or it can be a bottom-up movement. The top-down approach is led by established politicians or business people who believe they speak for the average person and they have the answers to solve the issues being faced. The bottom-up approach is when members of this community take a leadership position. A classic example would be Cesar Chavez who founded the National Farm Workers Association.

One perspective on the value of protests was best stated by the late great folk singer Pete Seeger. He stood up for every cause of his generation including nuclear power, women's rights and the environment. Pete said that despite his involvement in numerous causes over the years, he was not sure it made a difference, but it did let him meet the good people, those with good hearts.

Bottom Line - In 2016, voter frustration resulted in the election of a president who ran on a populist platform. There is a certain irony that the underclass used the ballot box to shake up the political scene and this led to massive protests by individuals who may be categorized as liberals. Perhaps we are living through that ancient Chinese curse - may we live in interesting times.

CHAPTER TWENTY-THREE

THE ROAD AHEAD

A strong family is like money in the bank

The landscape has changed. As manufacturing jobs disappear many blue-collar families are surviving by having both spouses employed in lower-paying jobs, such as retail or service, combined with the occasional use of the government safety net. They may own their home, but often have meager savings and live a pay day to pay day existence. They are one crisis short of being unable to pay their monthly expenses. Standard financial planning strategies include the use short-term survival techniques such as remortgaging the house and utilizing personal lines of credit. Relationships are disintegrating at an alarming rate and this is accelerating the financial issues. Two family incomes are replaced by two separate families. Child support payments have become either an additional expense or an obligation that is being ignored. Families lacking savings and private pensions will rely on government pensions during retirement.

Unless they are wealthy, many families will find maintaining their lifestyle a challenge in retirement if they do not have defined benefit pension plans. These plans are disappearing in the private sector and the other sources of retirement income may generate insufficient income. This problem will be magnified if individuals are making their investment decisions and their conservative or unsophisticated nature results in insufficient assets allocated to equities. If low interest rates are the new normal, then the combination of a low allocation of resources to equity plus low rates will not generate the necessary level of retirement income. The situation is compounded, as lack of retirement income must be combined with increased life expectancies. Inadequate resources are available to house and provide health care for these men and women in their final few years of life.

Many groups will require government assistance, but there is a lower percentage of the population paying taxes to support this growing underclass. Governments have inherited massive deficits and a decaying infrastructure which makes funding ongoing expenditures in areas such as health care, education and defense more challenging. This does not take into consideration the financial impact of fighting climate change. Protecting the environment while benefiting from the economic vitality of the resource sector will be an ongoing policy challenge.

If governments had kept their financial house in order when boomers were in charge, they would have more flexibility to address the issue of a growing underclass. There will be more calls to increase taxes on upper-income earners, but a tipping point may be reached when an overtaxed workforce says enough is enough. This can result in large businesses, professionals and wealthy families moving to more tax friendly jurisdictions.

Very few politicians are addressing the issue of the decline of the middle class. Voters want change, but there is no consensus of what change is necessary. There will be increased calls to transfer wealth from the haves to the have-nots. Political instability appears to be a part of our future and innocent victims are usually a byproduct of such unrest.

The boomers left a different world than the one they inherited from their parents. What if technological advancements continue and a fraction of the population can deliver all of the products and services that our society needs? Let's assume 75% of the working population can do all the work necessary and that number will continue to decrease in future years. Years ago, this was seen as some type of utopia with increased leisure time and wealth for all. However, on a more pragmatic basis, how will we share the wealth between the highly skilled that produce the output and the ever-increasing portion of the population that does not participate in wealth creation? It is one issue if there is an underclass that lacks the skills or the desire to work, but it is a different matter if there is no work to be performed because a small segment of the workforce can produce all the necessary output. Do we redistribute wealth through progressive taxation or will a new model be developed? Those who have money do not have a great record of sharing their wealth with those who have less.

Bottom Line – Many middle-class families will be challenged to finance a lengthy retirement unless they prioritize this financial planning objective throughout their life. A growing number of families will have no option but to have their retirement funded by an overextended government. This is retirement hell.

CHAPTER TWENTY-FOUR

A Final Thought

*My goal in life is to be as great a person
as my dogs believes that I am*

Can the middle class be restored to its glory days?
No. For many people, it will never get better than it is today
and someday we can look back on today as the good old
days.

ACKNOWLEDGEMENTS

I have been blessed to make a journey through life surrounded by friends and colleagues of intelligence, insight, and character. I value their ideas, knowledge, and opinions that have been included in the book. Interactions with these men and women of intelligence and character who shared their wisdom helped develop a worldview that has served me well. To Bart Sullivan and Frank Walsh, my close friends that were not only the sounding board for many ideas included in this book but reviewed the manuscript and provided valuable insight. I value the friendship of Jim Scott, a Vice-President of the 3M Company, who hired me and acted as a mentor throughout my career; I shall be eternally thankful.

Manufactured by Amazon.ca
Acheson, AB